SHALL I SAY A KISS?

SHALL I SAY A KISS?

The Courtship Letters
of a Deaf Couple
1936-1938

Lennard J. Davis, *Editor*

Preface by Gerald J. Davis

GALLAUDET UNIVERSITY PRESS

Washington, D.C.

GALLAUDET UNIVERSITY PRESS

Washington, DC 20002

© 1999 by Lennard Davis.

Printed in the United States of America

Library of Congress Cataloging-in-Publication Data

Davis, Morris Joseph, 1898–1981.
    Shall I say a kiss? : the courtship letters of a deaf couple,
    1936–1938 / Lennard J. Davis, editor ; preface by Gerald Davis.
        p.   cm.
    ISBN 1-56368-076-9 (hc. : alk. paper)
        1. Davis, Morris Joseph, 1898–1981—Correspondence.   2. Davis,
    Eva Weintrobe, 1911–1972—Correspondence.   3. Deaf—New York
    (State)—New York—Correspondence.   4. Deaf—England—
    Correspondence.   5. Courtship—New York (State)—New York.
    6. New York (N.Y.)—Biography.   I. Davis, Eva Weintrobe, 1911–
    1972.   II. Davis, Lennard J., 1949–   .   III. Title.
    HV2534.D38A3   1999
    362.4′2′00922—dc21
    [B]   98-51831
                                                                                  CIP

∞ *The paper used in this publication meets the minimum requirements of
American National Standard for Information Sciences—Permanence of Paper
for Printed Library Materials, ANSI Z39.48-1984.*

With deepest love and appreciation to
Morris Joseph Davis (1898–1981)
and Eva Weintrobe (1911–1972),
whose love made possible this book
and without whom there would
have been only silence.

CONTENTS

PREFACE   *ix*

INTRODUCTION
Before Crossing the Divide   *1*

"I Shall Not Rush into Things . . ."   29
AUGUST 25, 1936 TO NOVEMBER 3, 1937

"Wondering . . .
If Your Love Had Ever Been Deep"   97
NOVEMBER 11, 1937 TO APRIL 22, 1938

"Dear Eva of My Own"   123
MAY 3, 1938 TO AUGUST 25, 1938

EPILOGUE
The Ever After   163

PREFACE

Love and Misunderstanding

Gerald J. Davis

It is a difficult task to reconcile the parents I knew so well as I was growing up to the young man and woman who wrote these delicate negotiations of lovers. To all outward appearances, they are not the same people. My mother was twenty-six when the correspondence began and my father, thirty-eight. Much older now than they were then, I look back across the years and try to imagine how they must have felt. The woman, who appears so feisty and self-assured in her letters, must have been terrified of leaving the warm security of her family and venturing forth on a journey to the New World to take up housekeeping with a man who was little more than a stranger. It may well be that Eva Weintrobe and Morris Davis had not actually met more than four or five times before she sailed for the States to be married. As Eva writes, "I am taking a very big risk." Her hesitation was well-founded because, as it turned out, Eva never saw her mother again.

Morris, at the time of their correspondence, was living with his father in a cold-water flat in Brooklyn. It must have been an unrewarding existence. He had little money. His work consisted of long hours of drudgery. His social life, aside from the Deaf club, was probably less than satisfying. The prospect of marrying a young and beautiful bride was, no doubt, a consummation devoutly to be wished.

I do not know the young woman who wrote these letters. The mother I knew was a submissive and docile wife who rarely argued with or contradicted my father. Over the years of their marriage, the force of his personality must have come to dominate hers and place her in a subservient role. However, she did, from time to time, show flashes of that humor, strength, and self-confidence that resonate in her letters. I can't imagine my mother being coquettish, as when she writes, "Shall I say a kiss?" She was always the dutiful wife, even when she did not agree with my father's decisions. She didn't display any of the sharp-edged sense of humor that had her write, in response to Morris's suggestion that they marry in England and then have him go alone to America, with her following him after she had secured her visa, "It is allright for cricketeers [ballplayers] & film stars, but Jewish people never do things like this."

My mother was also self-reliant then, as she demonstrates when she writes that she has saved enough money to buy her own wedding dress. When I envision my mother, I do not picture her as self-reliant.

Only five of Morris's letters have survived. Where are the rest of his letters, we wonder? Where are his long-winded protestations of love and his detailed pages of instructions? What did he say to kindle my mother's interest? We can only speculate that he was the more emotional and sentimental partner who saved Eva's letters while she discarded most of his as not worthy of preserving for posterity. What did he say to woo her and convince her that he was the one to marry? What declaration of affection persuaded her to give up the infamous "Leeds boy" and travel to New York to marry Morris? He seems to be the one pursuing the relationship at all costs, the one with the largest stack of emotional coins to lose. I cannot imagine my father as the ardent suitor. His personality was far from that of the gentle lover.

It was a given in our family that my father was smarter than my mother, but one could be convinced otherwise by these letters. His letters go on without many memorable phrases, while hers are sharp, to the point, and perhaps more skillfully written. Hers are certainly more fun to read, as reflected in her saucy retort to him, "Did you expect me to propose first?"

Morris's declaration of love and his proposal of marriage came soon after the onset of the correspondence. This was not at variance with his nature, which was somewhat impulsive. But Eva's strong-willed comments like "You have no right to balance my love for you in whether I go to America with you or not" and "Nothing will make me change my mind" surprise me and make me wonder what she was like as a young woman. She certainly was not like that as a mature woman, when she rarely exerted her will. However, when Eva says, "I will be a good wife to you," I know that her promise and prophesy were to come true as the marriage ripened into old age.

It is interesting to note the range of emotions—from anger to love, from joy to bitter disappointment—that these letters contain. Eva is shocked by Morris's impulsive actions in asking favors of her relatives and is proud when she scolds him, "I wonder what our relatives think of us now." I cannot recall ever seeing my mother shocked, since she always retained her sense of pride and dignity in front of others. I often thought of her as a regal person who, in my mind, bore a striking resemblance to Queen Elizabeth.

The thread that carries through from these letters to the people I knew as my parents is the expression of emotion. My mother was a reticent person and was reluctant to make a great display of her emotions, whereas my father was more openly demonstrative of affection and, possibly, more in need of expressions of love.

Now, as I re-read their correspondence, I am drawn back into the dim recesses of memory as I become a child again, recalling what it was like to journey through a Deaf world. Images, sounds and people rise from the past to reassert their places in my consciousness. Events I hadn't thought of in years become as fresh as yesterday's newspaper.

Eva became deaf at the age of six. When I was a child, I was told that she had fallen over backwards in a rocking chair and had hit her head, and that was the cause of her deafness. I later learned that she had contracted meningitis, from which she recovered fully except for the loss of her hearing. When she became deaf, she already had facility of speech (with a delightful English accent from the town of her birth, Liverpool), so she was able to make herself understood to the hearing world with little difficulty.

Morris, on the other hand, became deaf when he was eighteen months old. The family myth held that his teenage aunt had dropped him down a flight of stairs. It wasn't until many years later that I saw the scars behind his ears and learned that an operation had been performed upon him when he was an infant. The exact nature of his childhood illness was shrouded in mystery, but the butchery of the turn-of-the-century English medicine was evident because he told me that both of his eardrums had been removed by a surgeon.

For some unexplained reason, it was considered shameful to become deaf through illness, as if it were somehow the fault of the patient. If one became deaf through an accident, that is to say suddenly and because of an external shock, it was not quite as much of a stigma. I never knew if this was a prejudice of our family alone or if other deaf families shared the same belief.

My father's speech was difficult for hearing people to comprehend because he had never heard the sounds that words made. His manner of speaking was coarse and guttural, but he had a keen intelligence that he was not bashful about displaying. If I made a mistake in sign language, he was sure to correct me vehemently. This was his territory and he was the guide, the expert tracker and wagon master.

As soon as I could talk, I became the emissary through whom my parents were able to communicate with the hearing world. And so a child assumed adult responsibilities.

It was a mixed blessing. I felt important because of the power that language gave me as the key to enter the grown-up world. But I also felt embarrassed because of my parents' disability. This embarrassment was a continual and unwelcome companion on my travels around New York City with my mother and father. I wasn't ashamed of them in the safety of our home, but I dreaded those trips on the subway and pretended that I wasn't traveling with that deaf couple seated next to me who were conversing in sign language, an event that engendered great curiosity among the other passengers.

When I was four years old, I locked my mother in a

closet. I don't remember why I did it. We were alone in our three-room apartment in the Bronx, and my mother was cleaning out a clothes closet. I slammed the door shut and stood there listening to her frantic repeated cries of "Gerald! Please open the door! Turn the doorknob!" There was no way to open the door from the inside of the closet. Picture this helpless woman, deaf to her surroundings, now deprived of her most important sense and enclosed in the closet's darkness. As the story was recounted to me later, I finally opened the door after about ten or fifteen minutes and was greeted with a hug, not a spanking. Such was the loving nature of this woman.

The occupations open to deaf people at that time were few. Most of my parents' friends were tailors or printers. One was a teacher of deaf students. Since he did not have to work with his hands, he was granted a measure of respect.

My father was a tailor. He would wake up at 5 o'clock each morning to go to work. He had an electric alarm clock with a plug-in cord attached to a buzzer. This buzzer, which he put under his pillow, would vibrate to wake him when the alarm went off. He would then wake my mother to prepare his breakfast while he shaved.

My mother was a seamstress. She seemed to be working constantly as I was growing up. I remember that her hands were always in motion, always in the process of producing something, whether a garment or a meal. When my brother and I were young, she worked at home. Wealthy ladies (or so I considered them) would come to our small flat to be fitted and measured for garments. My mother would get down on her knees, pins in her mouth, to ensure that the hems of the dresses were level with the ground. The ladies would nod and smile and gesture, "Very good."

Almost every week, usually on a Sunday afternoon, my parents took me to the Deaf club. The Deaf club met in a large empty room in a community center, with folding tables and chairs leaning against the stark brick walls. There were always games and cheap toys and candy for the children. The members were invariably friendly, and I played with the hearing children of these deaf adults. I can't recall any deaf children and I wonder now why there were none. We, parents and children, sat on metal folding chairs and watched American movies with English subtitles shown on a folding screen by a 16-millimeter projector, which often broke down and left burn holes in the film. The Deaf club to a hearing boy was a quiet world of flying hands, occasional grunts, and clacking teeth. As I grew older, my visits to the Deaf club became less frequent, but my mother and father went every week without fail. The Deaf club was their haven and the nexus of their social life. It was a meeting place, a support group, and a communications center, since many of the deaf did not have a telephone or a TTY during the years I was growing up. Some of these people had been my parents' friends from early childhood in England, and some of these friendships had lasted for seventy-five years.

Perhaps it is ironic, but my father bought me my first phonograph. A man who couldn't hear went into a music store and bought a portable record player and a forty-five single of Patti Page singing "How Much Is That Doggie in the Window?" It was a rudimentary machine. Its sound wasn't very clear, but it played music loudly—and that was enough for a young, undemanding child.

The appearance of a television set in our home in 1950 was a significant event. That Emerson console became the centerpiece of our evenings. Before my father purchased the television, my entertainment was an Emerson radio that sat on our kitchen table. My father always knew when the radio had been turned on contrary to his wishes, even when I had shut it off, because he would place his hand on top of the radio and feel the heat from the vacuum tubes, which was a telltale giveaway.

Our family signed up for telephone service in 1956. Before then we would use the phone of a neighbor across the hallway if we needed to make an important call. A new responsibility was added to my list: I now had to make all the phone calls that heretofore other people had placed for my parents. My father would dictate the script and stand in front of me to read my lips and ensure that I repeated his words exactly.

I remember the last time I had to interpret for my father. It was at a union hearing before an arbitration panel to present my father's case for some allegedly unjustified vacation days he had taken. There was some dispute as to whether he was entitled to the time off and vacation pay. I was a man by then, and for the first time felt like one as I translated his words. My father was as persuasive and as long-winded in presenting his case as he had been in his letters. The panel ruled in his favor. We had been a team, and a successful one.

I cannot recall my parents ever complaining about their deafness. To them it was a fact of life, like eating or breathing. They were simply healthy, intelligent human beings who did not have the function of hearing. Their lives were full, but had one quality different from the lives of hearing people: their existence was in a Deaf world, encircled by the hearing one. I grew up in that Deaf world, but I left it behind when I became an adult. And now this fortuitous discovery of long-forgotten letters gives me a welcome opportunity to see my mother and father in a new way.

INTRODUCTION

Before Crossing the Divide

Lennard J. Davis

When Morris Davis, my father, died in 1981, at the age of eighty-two, he had been ill with cancer for ten years. My mother, Eva, had died nine years earlier, at the age of sixty-two, in a traffic accident. Both were profoundly deaf. The last time I saw my father alive, he was barely conscious. I shook him, the way I used to do when I was a child, wanting him to wake up on Sunday morning and play with me. He barely opened his eyes. I signed "How are you?" Feebly, he replied, "Fine, thank you." By the next morning he had died.

After the funeral, my brother and I went to clear his possessions from the apartment in which he had lived. Most of his papers had to do with racewalking. He had held the unofficial American record for walking 25 miles, a record of which he was very proud, and about which he told almost any visitor or passerby.

But among his clippings, medals, and trophies, we found a small packet, neatly tied up. It contained a series of letters—mostly from my mother, then Eva Weintrobe—still in their envelopes and arranged in chronological order. I took these home to look at them more carefully.

That night, I settled into my bed and opened the first envelope. The neatly written letter, yellowed with age, was from my mother and was dated August 23, 1936, two years before their marriage. It began, "Dear Morris, It was indeed a surprise for me to receive your card & I shall say a pleasant surprise too." This was the first of many letters between my mother and father. In this first one, the signs of courtship are detectable—the blush of surprise, the pleasure of an interest requited. This beginning was for Eva and Morris, as for billions of other humans, the first instance when affection and even love seem possible. And like so many other moments, it could have gone awry. Indeed, the letters that followed, the letters that I read avidly and voyeuristically for several nights in a row, always teetered at the edge of disaster. Each letter sowed the seeds of their courtship's destruction as well as its creation.

Eva and Morris tried, over the course of two complicated years, to understand each other and forge a relationship through letters. Because these two were separated—initially by being in different cities, then by being in different countries—they had to accomplish in writing what most people work out in person. They had their fights, their reconciliations, their declarations of love and disappointment within the pages of these letters, which flew between the United States and Britain as silent emissaries. My parents were Pyramus and Thisbe, separated by distance but passing notes through a chink in the transatlantic wall.

As an English professor who specialized in eighteenth-century novels, I had read many epistolary romances. I was used to the slow unfolding that these stories in letters, like Richardson's *Clarissa* or Rousseau's *La Nouvelle Héloïse,* held in store. But reading my own parents' letters added a different element. Now, the fate of the hero and heroine contained my fate as well. And like the Greeks who experienced catharsis while watching *Oedipus,* even though they knew how it would conclude, I too winced and shuddered at each twist and turn of fate, although I knew very well the end. When, several times, Eva and Morris decided to break off the relationship, I felt myself begin to evaporate, grow translucent, and fade into nonexistence, only to return to life in the next letter, in which my parents reconciled.

I read the letters late into the nights, following Morris and Eva's understandings and misunderstandings, disagreements and declarations of affection, until I reached the last one, written almost two years after the first, in which my mother wrote: "This I think will be my last letter to you before I leave England. I can hardly believe it is true." And with the end of separation came the end of the writing. But in the meantime, I had become that magical third party—the reader, who wants the star-crossed couple to be reunited and in the course to become my parents and create my life. But my collaboration as reader had no willing co-conspirator in an omniscient author. My parents' reunion became the point of my separation from their intimate thoughts and feelings. I wanted to know more, but the letters had ended. What happened when Eva arrived in America? What was their meeting like? What happened once they were married? All I had was my recollection of their stories recounted later, casual and censored, about this period in their lives. The authentic voices they had created in writing, their literate, thoughtful ways, had fallen silent.

The experience of reading the letters was profoundly moving. I was able to see my parents not as the archetypes of Mother and Father they had become over time, but as relatively young people, substantially younger than I am now, trying to understand how their lives might fit together. Rather than the passive, quiet mother I remember, who toiled long hours at housekeeping while working as a seamstress, I found a strong, energetic woman with a clear sense of her desires. I was impressed by the way my mother could write so directly and forcefully about her wishes and plans. Instead of the sometimes gruff and tense man I had grown up loving and fearing, my father was the suitor urgently pleading for love and affection. I was touched by his need to read words of desire and encouragement. And I was swept up in the drama—Morris writing from America asking Eva in England to leave her family, take an ocean liner, and give up everything for their new life together. In my head were images of Leslie Howard and Greer Garson, Laurence Olivier and Joan Fontaine, black-and-white films of England in the 1930s with beautiful heroines whose eyes twinkle with mischief and handsome men with dimpled chins, pencil-thin moustaches, and elegant ways.

After I read the letters, I gave them to my brother to read. He had a similar experience, which we shared with each other. Then we put the letters away. More than fifteen years passed, and again I began to think about the letters. In those fifteen years, I had gone through a process of finding again my Deaf identity by attending Children of Deaf Adults (CODA) meetings, writing about deafness, and become reinvolved in

Deaf and disability-related activities.[1] With this new awareness, I began to think that such a collection of letters might be useful to scholars and historians of Deaf culture. My first thought was to donate the letters to Gallaudet University's library. But then I wondered if there might be a broader appeal to Deaf and hearing readers. My brother and I discussed the matter, I talked with Gallaudet University Press, and *Shall I Say a Kiss? The Courtship Letters of a Deaf Couple, 1936–1938* is the result.

Why would anyone, other than family members, want to read this correspondence? I had to ask myself this question since I am opening a private affair to public scrutiny. There is no scandal here; no act of perfidy or outrage. My parents were just ordinary, working-class people involved in a courtship. Of course, their deafness adds an element of interest for some readers. Yet, their letters have a scholarly value of which my parents themselves would have been unaware. Their correspondence provides documentary evidence of the life of two working-class, Jewish, British, Deaf people in the 1930s. My father's preservation of this material allowed for a relatively rare phenomenon—the consistent, journal-like account of the "lived" experience of Deaf people over a period of time. The account would have been more complete had my mother saved letters as assiduously as had my father.[2] But, because she did not, the record of my father's writing is much more meager.

---

1. I recount this rediscovery in my memoir, *My Sense of Silence: A Memoir of a Childhood with Deafness* (Champaign: University of Illinois Press, 1999).

2. One is tempted to speculate about why Eva did not save Morris's letters. Was it that he valued the letters more than she did? Or was it simply that, because she had to travel to America, she could not bring all her possessions?"

Since the correspondence is mainly composed of my mother's writing, it also is a record of the life and opinions of a young, working-class, Deaf woman about to embark on marriage. Eva's conflicts are particularly illuminating since she had to work through various practical, ethical, and disability-related issues. She had to decide whether or not to marry a man with whom she had gone out only three or four times, whether to leave her family in Liverpool and venture across the Atlantic to follow this relatively unknown man who insistently begged her to come. Her problem was compounded by her deafness because the U.S. Immigration Act of 1924 had already been implemented, setting national quotas and stringent requirements for entry visas. These requirements included medical and de facto racial barriers that she had to overcome—both for her deafness and her Jewish descent.

In publishing these letters, one also has to take into consideration issues of personal privacy. I am sure that if my parents were alive, they would not be comfortable with my revealing these letters to the eyes of others, particularly nonfamily members. However, at the same time, I am sure they would be honored, although somewhat puzzled, that Gallaudet University Press was their publisher. My parents did not have more than a primary-school education, and the ways of academia were always a bit mysterious to them.

In asking who would want to read these letters, I also have to ask another question. What does "deafness" have to do with this correspondence? On a simple level, the answer would be *everything*. Both Morris and Eva were deaf as well as Deaf, that is, having a physical inability to hear but also being fully integrated into Deaf culture and language. But what will strike most readers is that these letters do not seem "Deaf" in any way. The correspondence is written in a clear, readable style, and for the most part does not contain the kind of grammatical structures that would suggest sign-language word order or the inability to translate from sign language to English.[3]

This absence of Deaf issues in the correspondence will strike hearing people oddly. They will perhaps want there to be more about what they think of as a totalizing disability. But one of the lessons of these letters is that to Morris and Eva their deafness was so much a part of their lives it did not require constant discussion and attention. Like fish, they did not have to discover water. Just as outsiders demand that films and literature about gays, African Americans, and so on be "about" the identity issue, so too might hearing readers seek to find their normality confirmed by the fact that "abnormals" can think of nothing else but their putative "lack." There is no such luck here. Morris's and Eva's lives, like anyone else's, include references to friends and family. All the friends mentioned are Deaf people, but their deafness is not highlighted.

Deafness may show up thematically in one area. Over and over again, Eva and Morris both say that they wish to avoid "misunderstanding," as Eva does on June 28, 1938, when she writes: "I hope from now on we will both never have any more uncertainties & misunderstanding." As Deaf people

---

3. The quality of the letter-writing may be the result of combined factors. Both my parents attended the Residential School for the Jewish Deaf in London, an institution that, along with other Jewish deaf schools, was somewhat elite, typically schooling children from families with some financial resources. Also, one can speculate that the culture emphasized letter-writing in a way that differs from the way we do now. In the manner that ordinary soldiers during the Civil War were known to write eloquent and moving letters, so too my parents, with their elementary education, may have felt the necessity of putting their best words forward in letters.

who have lived a life filled with the vexed problem of communication—problems between themselves and hearing relatives, friends, and officials—they are acutely aware of the difficulty in getting things right, passing along the message accurately. So when Morris and Eva are forced into negotiating their entire relationship through writing, they want to get it right. Often when things go wrong, they take special efforts to see that misunderstandings do not occur again.

Some biographical information may be in order here. Eva Weintrobe was born in Liverpool, England, on September 3, 1911. Her father, Elihu Weintrobe, was born in 1876 in Nowogrod, Poland. His lineage can be traced back to one Szmul born in 1738 in Poland.[4] Elihu was originally named Eliasz Leib Chmielewski, but he took the family name of his mother, Sule Badana Weintraub, who was born in 1851. He may have taken his mother's name when he emigrated to England, thinking Weintraub (or Weintrobe) sounded less foreign. Elihu's father was Joseph Chmielewski, born in Myszyniec, Poland, near Nowogrod, in 1854. Eva's mother, Leah, was also from this region.

My mother lived her early life in Liverpool on Moon Street, a street near the Anglican cathedral in a then Jewish neighborhood. The street was subsequently demolished during World War II. Her father was a cabinetmaker who later opened a small grocery shop. She had two older brothers, Joseph and Max, and two sisters—an elder, Celia, and a younger,

---

4. I have my cousin Sheila Salo to thank for her extensive genealogical research that allowed me to know a bit about my mother's family history.

Betty. The family was not poor, but certainly not middle-class. In 1918, just before the family moved to a new house on Chattam Street, with electricity rather than the gaslight they previously had used, Eva, seven years old, contracted spinal meningitis. She was expected to die. Doctors shaved her head and packed her in ice water, and she managed to pull through. She remembered watching the children go to school from the balcony of the hospital, but hiding from them because she was embarrassed by her shorn head. It was when her mother came to visit, chatting with her, that she realized she could no longer hear. The family took her to all kinds of doctors. Each promised cures but never produced any hearing.

My mother quickly adapted to being deaf. She was sent to London to the Residential School for the Jewish Deaf, where she learned to read and to write. Although the school was oralist in orientation, she learned to sign by association with the children there. She continued at this school until she was about sixteen. She told me that she was always afraid that she would not be able to go home on holidays because she was pale. So when the children were lined up for inspection, she would pinch her cheeks to appear rosy and healthy and thus get permission to go home.

As she grew up, her Deaf friends formed the core of her social world. They were an energetic, athletic crew and spent much of their time on trips to the beach. I have many photos of Eva from this period looking tan and trim. One place she enjoyed going was to Hailbi Island, which was only accessible when the tide was low. She and her friends would get up early and return late, although they did have mishaps in which they were stranded on the island when the tide came in too quickly. Eva worked at Lewis's department store as a seamstress

*Eva (lower left)
with Deaf friends
at the beach.*

*Eva (seated third from left) on an excursion
to Hailbi Island.*

and also helped out in the family grocery store. That was her life until she met my father.

My father, Morris Joseph Davis, was born in 1898 in the Whitechapel section of London, a poor, Jewish neighborhood. His Yiddish name was Moishe Yussel, but he preferred his anglicized name. His parents were hearing, as were his three siblings, Natalie, Jane, and Abraham. His father, Solomon Davis, was a fishmonger and his mother, Bella Esther Moskowitz, was the daughter of a rabbi. Both of them were born in Poland and had emigrated to England in the nineteenth century. Solomon left Bella for New York in the early 1910s and the couple never reunited, although they never divorced either. The reasons for his departure are uncertain. I have heard three reasons; any and all may have been true. First, he and his wife were incompatible; second, he killed a man in the boxing ring during a prize fight; and third, he was in debt and about to be arrested.

Morris either was born deaf or became deaf through illness prelingually. We have conflicting stories about his becoming deaf. On the one hand, there is the story that his aunt dropped him while carrying him down the stairs. There is also the story of his playing quietly on the floor while his uncle fiddled on the violin; the uncle suddenly realized that Morris was deaf because he did not react to the music. A final story tells of an operation in which both his eardrums were removed to cure an inner-ear infection. How these stories fit together is not clear, and what we have amounts more to a mythology than a reality.[5]

Morris grew up in an impoverished household.

---

5. I provide more details in *My Sense of Silence*.

Eva at her home around the time she first met Morris.

He attended the Residential School for the Jewish Deaf in London as a charity student and helped to support his family first as a carpenter's apprentice and later as a tailor's apprentice. His family lived in a single room above the fishmonger's shop. After Morris's father left the family, his mother earned money by selling fabrics door-to-door. At that point the family was so poor they only had one good meal on the Sabbath. Bella would give each child a small drop of liquor, which she measured from a thimble worn around her neck, so that they would be able to hold the food down. My father tried to better his lot through gambling, but he ended up losing most of his money. In an effort to reform himself, he also began to participate in boxing and walking races. The latter became his passion, and he was eventually accepted into the prestigious London Polytechnic Harriers, in which he was a teammate of Harold Abrahams, whose life is depicted in the film *Chariots of Fire*.

Morris followed his father to New York in 1924. In New York, Morris continued his racing feats. He joined the 92nd Street Young Men's Hebrew Association's track and field team, composed of the best Jewish athletes in New York. He was the only deaf athlete to make the team. Although Morris attempted to join the New York Athletic Club, the equivalent of the London Polytechnic Harriers, he was always barred both for being deaf and for being Jewish. Nevertheless, Morris won many events for the "Y" and held the unofficial American record for 25 miles. He did all this while working as a sewing-machine operator in ladies' coats and suits in the garment district.

Morris returned to England in 1935 and stayed with his mother in London. He journeyed up to Liverpool in August

Morris (center) with his father, Solomon, and mother, Bella.

1936, and at a dance at the Warrington Deaf Club, he met my mother. At that time, he was thirty-eight and she was twenty-five. According to his later account, he had seen a photograph of Eva while he was in London and went to Liverpool with the express purpose of meeting her. After they had danced a few times, he decided he wanted to marry her.

The first letter of the correspondence refers to that meeting, and the following letters indicate that they saw each other only about four times before he asked her to marry him. Obviously, this haste was confusing to Eva, and much of the correspondence initially deals with her reluctance to plunge into a marriage with a man she barely knew. She was concerned about his ability to find employment (since he had left his job as a sewing-machine operator to return to England for this long vacation), although she repeatedly says that she did not care about money.

Early on issues about immigration arose. Eva worried that her entering the United States would not be as easy as Morris said. Morris's visa was about to run out, so he proposed that Eva go to America with him, but she wanted to become engaged first. She asked him either to prolong his stay in England or, if he could not, to go back to the United States as an engaged man. After much debating, Morris left in June 1937, and his urgent pleas that Eva leave with him became demands that she come over to marry him as quickly as possible.

Eva mentions in a letter (August 22, 1937) the case of a deaf man who could not get a visa to America because "he is deaf" and worried that she would have trouble as well. This is the first time in the correspondence that deafness comes up as an issue. As Eva pursued the visa, she realized that the reluc-

Morris (left) with his father (right) in New York City at the annual city hall to Coney Island walking race in November 1935.

Morris (second row, left) with the 92nd Street YMHA track and field team.

tance of the American consulate to grant her a visa was largely owing to her deafness, although the consulate never mentioned this point directly.

In order to understand Eva's difficulty in obtaining a visa, we have to consider the history of immigration policy in the United States. When my father arrived in America in the early 1920s, there were no quotas on European immigration, although the national debate had heated up over the vexing problem of the tired, poor, huddled masses of foreigners flowing into the United States. But by 1937, when Eva tried to obtain a visa, immigration laws had changed.

In 1907 Congress established an immigration commission that concluded the recent immigration of Eastern European Jews, Poles, Bohemians, Russians, and Italians, adding to the older wave of Scandinavians, Irish, and Germans, had had an unsalutory influence on American society. By 1910 southern and eastern Europeans made up nearly 77 percent of the total immigration to the United States.[6] The Commission recommended a literacy test as a screen against undesirables. Presidents Taft and Wilson vetoed the legislation, but Congress overrode Wilson's veto in 1917, riding a crest of prewar tensions to institute a literacy test.

The wording of the 1907 legislation clearly links ethnicity, race, class, and disability by advocating the exclusion of

idiots, imbeciles, feeble-minded persons, epileptics [along with] . . . paupers, vagrants, persons likely to

---

6. See Margret Winzer, *The History of Special Education: From Isolation to Integration* (Washington, D.C.: Gallaudet University Press, 1993), 303.

> become public charges, . . . persons afflicted with tu-
> berculosis or with a loathsome or contagious disease
> . . . polygamists, anarchists . . . prostitutes, persons
> . . . who are found to be and are certified by the exam-
> ining surgeon as being mentally or physically defec-
> tive, such mental or physical defect being of such a
> nature as to affect the ability of the alien to earn a
> living.[7]

Although this language had not yet been translated into immigration law, people with disabilities were often denied entry
into the United States. Luckily, Morris was not affected by the
motives behind this language when he came to the U.S.

Nonetheless, documents concerning immigration rou-
tinely blurred race, health, class, and morality. Jews, for example, were seen as medically inferior as well as socially un-
desirable. In a 1937 book by Otmar Freiherr von Verschuer,
director of the Frankfurt Institute for Racial Hygiene, Jews
are shown to be more prone to diabetes, flatfeet, staggers (tor-
sionsdystonie), hemophilia, xeroderma pigmentosum, deafness, and nervous disorders than non-Jews.[8] But these notions

---

7. Paul Popeno and Roswell Hill Johnson, *Applied Eugenics* (New York:
Macmillan, 1918).

8. See Robert Proctor, *Racial Hygiene: Medicine under the Nazis* (Cam-
bridge: Harvard University Press, 1988), 197. While the Nazis are now popularly
remembered as the foremost proponents of eugenics, the greatest proponents and
developers of eugenic theory were the British and North Americans. The work of
Sir Francis Galton in England and Charles Davenport in the United States laid the
foundations for the study of eugenics, and the United States and the United Kingdom developed and pursued legislation with eugenic aims far earlier than the Germans. For more information on this subject, see my *Enforcing Normalcy: Disability, Deafness, and the Body* (New York: Verso, 1996), 23–49; Daniel Kevles, *In*

linking race and biology were by no means limited to the Nazis. This opinion governed U.S. immigration policy during this period. For example, Dr. J. G. Wilson, a U.S. Public Health Service doctor who examined immigrants coming through Ellis Island, wrote in *Popular Science Monthly,* "If the science of eugenics deserves any practical application at all, it should insist upon a careful study of the . . . Jews" because "the Jews are a highly inbred and psychopathically inclined race" whose defects are "almost entirely due to heredity."[9] Harry H. Laughlin, who served as an advisor to the Immigration Commission and was an assistant to Charles Davenport's Eugenics Records Office, defined the socially inadequate as "feebleminded, insane, criminalistic, diseased, blind, deaf, deformed, and dependent including orphans, ne'er-do-wells, the homeless, tramps and paupers."[10] The notion that immigrants like Jews would bring in inferior genetic material that could lead to deafness, for example, encouraged further restrictions on immigration. Alexander Graham Bell, who had inveighed against deaf intermarriage, which he feared would create a "deaf variety of the human race," also saw immigration in general as a threat to American genetic purity. He warned that the American citizen was "surrounded by prolific immigrant races ready to take its place," and there appeared "a serious danger" that the native race would be "displaced by the immigrants."[11]

---

the Name of Eugenics: Genetics and the Uses of Human Heredity (New York: Alfred Knopf, 1985); and Martin Pernick, *The Black Stork: Eugenics and the Death of "Defective" Babies in American Medicine and Motion Pictures since 1915* (New Brunswick, N.J.: Rutgers University Press, 1963).

9. Cited in Pernick, *Black Stork,* 56.

10. See Haller, *Eugenics,* 133.

11. Cited in Winzer, *History of Special Education,* 304.

The literacy requirement enacted by Congress did not effectively limit immigration. And in the postwar period, in which heightened Americanism combined with the Red Scare, the Immigration Act of 1924 was passed by Congress and signed by President Harding. The act limited immigration to 3 percent of the foreign-born of each nationality in the United States according to the 1910 census and capped the total number of immigrants at 150,000 after 1927.[12]

It was with this nationalistic, ableist bias in immigration policy that Eva had to contend. She had three strikes against her since she was working-class, Jewish, and deaf. The "List or Manifest of Alien Passengers for the United States Immigrant Inspector at Port of Arrival"[13] for the SS *Scythia,* on which my mother arrived, is a document that is indicative of the biased U.S. immigration policy. Questions that the U.S. government inspector had to ask "alien passengers" include: "Ever in prison or almshouse, or institution for the care and treatment of the insane, or supported by charity?" "Whether a polygamist?" "Whether an anarchist?" "Whether a person who believes in or advocates the overthrow by force or violence the government of the United States or all forms of law, etc. . . . ?" "Condition of health, mental and physical?" and "Deformed or crippled. Nature, length of time, and cause." In my mother's entry is written "med cert deafness bilateral." Under "Marks of identification" is written "Deaf." In addition to her deafness, under the category of "nationality" is written "Britain," but under "Race or people" she is listed as "He-

---

12. See Haller, *Eugenics,* 157. Haller also points out that no Asians of any nationality were allowed to immigrate.

13. I have to thank Sheila Salo again for finding this document.

brew." The Christian passenger below her on the list is listed also as "Britain" but under "Race" is listed as "English." As far as entry quotas were concerned, my mother was to be considered "Hebrew" even though she and her parents were British citizens.

There was a continuum, obvious in this document, that linked being working-class, insane, deaf, disabled, and so on, as Laughlin had suggested. Since many Eastern European Jews were also seen as political radicals, being an anarchist was seen as a racially defined category.[14] And since being Jewish was considered a category of medical disability as well, we can see how difficult it was for Eva to jump the barrier of immigration law and enter the United States. Also interesting is the fact that Eva's deafness was seen as a "mark of identification" even though deafness is not visible. Rather, and to the point, deafness was seen as a mark, a brand, a confirmation of undesirability in aliens. Given this level of discrimination, we can see how difficult it was for Eva to have surmounted the barrier set up by the immigration laws, written and de facto, in order to join Morris.

I do not think that Eva considered her being Jewish decisive in her problems obtaining a visa. Although anti-Semitism must have been quite prevalent, Eva tended to live in a Jewish enclave both in Liverpool and then in residential school. Although her family was Orthodox, as was Morris's, and Jewish life played an important part in their world, the

---

14. Anarchy had been referred to by a writer in a business magazine fifty years earlier as "a blood disease" of "communistic and revolutionary races." Cited in John Higham, *Strangers in the Land: Patterns of American Nativism, 1860–1925* (1955; reprint, New Brunswick, N.J.: Rutgers University Press, 1994), 138.

move toward assimilation was strong in her generation. My Uncle Joe, who was an Orthodox rabbi, kept the religion, but his appearance, aside from a discreet, black skull cap, was like any of his British compeers. My mother's letters refer to elaborate preparations for holidays. In our household in New York she kept a kosher home and made time-consuming dishes, including her own gefilte fish, pickled herring, and so on, but she was not overwhelmingly concerned with religion. Neither of my parents went to synagogue, although this probably was because at that time there were no sign language services available for Deaf people.

Eva's encounters with the consulate general indicate that it was her deafness, and not her Jewishness, that proved the stumbling block. She was told to come to London on October 12, 1937, after all her papers were completed, and she did. But her letter of October 14 details how she had "come back from the Consulate very disappointed whereas I had gone with great hopes." She underwent a medical examination, as required by law, but then was told that she would not get a visa. It seems clear in retrospect that until Eva arrived in London, the consul general had no way of knowing she was deaf. Yet, since the medical examination clearly specified her deafness, as the SS *Scythia*'s passenger manifest indicated, it seems equally clear that the findings of this examination probably had the effect of closing the iron door for a time. A letter from the consul dated November 3, 1937, required more proof of support from relatives, the implications being that a deaf woman entering the United States would automatically become a charge to the state if left on her own, and that deafness was equated with inability to work.

In response, Morris immediately wrote to the Immigration and Naturalization Service in the United States and received a reply on October 29, 1937, in which Henry Hazard, assistant to the commissioner, bureaucratically laid out many of the provisions of the Immigration Act of 1924. Hazard noted that both parties were deaf and warned Morris that even if he went back to England and married Eva, there was no guarantee that she could get a permanent visa. He noted that while marriage gave the applicant a nonquota status, so Eva could enter despite quota levels, it did not rule out refusal for medical reasons, for example. The letter is clearly meant to be discouraging, embodying as it does Hazard's ableist attitudes concerning deaf people.

In response to these events, Morris did two drastic things. He went to Eva's uncle, Arthur Winarick, who was then the owner of the barber-supply business that made Jerris hair products, and asked Winarick to pay for his passage back to England to marry my mother.[15] He then wrote my mother, telling her to be ready to marry him in three weeks. Eva's response was definitive. She cabled him telling him not to come and followed the cable with a letter in which she conveyed her astonishment at his effrontery in approaching her uncle for money without informing her. Under the circumstances, Eva said, she no longer wished to marry Morris.

However, this misunderstanding was patched up in subsequent letters. Meanwhile, Morris had sent another letter to the consulate general saying he was coming to marry Eva,

---

15. Arthur Winarick, married to my grandfather's sister Rivka (anglicized to Regina, then shortened to Jean) Chmielewski, later became the owner of the Concord Hotel in the Catskills. We were told he was among the 100 richest men in America. It was rumored in our family that his initial wealth was derived from bootleg alcohol, which he diverted from the manufacture of his hair tonic.

and the response, detailed by my mother in a letter of December 16, 1937, amounted to another bureaucratic reflex asking again that my mother initiate paperwork. As Eva writes:

> I had a letter from the Consulate but it seems that you did not explain that I had previously applied for a visa as he instructed me to send papers to you for affidavits & letters from your bank & place of employment. I am afraid it is useless to write to the Consulate as it is very hard to make them change.

Her resignation seems appropriate considering the discrimination inherent in the immigration laws and the sole decision-making power held by the consul general. She later states that she "had been refused [a visa] through my deafness."

Then suddenly, without warning, on February 2, 1938, Eva wrote a letter to Morris breaking off the relationship, saying she realized she did not want to go to America. In a subsequent letter she explains that a deaf man from Leeds, Isadore Alpers, had begun courting her, and her family, not wanting Eva to leave the country, supported Alpers. However, by dating Alpers, Eva came to the realization that the man she really wanted to marry was Morris, and this clear understanding seems to be a turning point in the relationship. She no longer was in doubt. After some misgivings on his part, Morris forgave her.

The immigration plan Morris now proposed was to have Eva apply for a visitor's visa and stay with her relatives. After a short time, Morris and Eva would be married. She would then go to Canada and apply for a permanent visa. Morris, in his ardor, glosses over the warning given to him by the U.S. Immigration and Naturalization Service that being married is no guarantee of being able to receive a permanent visa. Meanwhile, in a letter dated April 22, 1938, the consul general, Douglas Jenkins, informs Eva that although he has received Arthur Winarick's affidavit, "Mr. Winarick has failed to prove his alleged income and savings." That affidavit, dated February 14, 1938, lists Arthur Winarick as born in Russia and having a net worth of "all totalling over $500,000." Clearly, Douglas Jenkins was dubious about this Russian Jew who claimed so much wealth. A further clarification from Morris's sister Janie, who went to speak with the consul general, indicates that Winarick had to ask his banker to send a letter confirming his wealth and had to supply another letter from some "authority" stating the weekly income of his business.

At last, when all the affidavits were received, Eva went to the consulate and finally got her visa. As she describes it:

> I went through it all alone but was not a bit nervous. After being examined by a doctor I was taken into the Consulate's Office, at first I thought it was Mr. Jenkins, but he signed his name on my papers as Mr. Colebrook[.] [T]owards the end of my interview with him another man came in[.] I guessed it was Mr. Jenkins although I was not told his name, he smiled to me & jokingly asked if I was not already married. After I had my visa & was on my way out I met him again & I thanked him personally.

This moment, when Eva Weintrobe meets Douglas Jenkins, is worthy of consideration. Eva, the poor, Jewish, deaf twenty-seven-year-old woman, ventures into the American consulate and meets Consul General Douglas Jenkins, aged fifty-eight. Douglas Jenkins was the "other man" in this love story. He in effect controls the fates of both Eva and Morris. *Who Was Who* tells us a bit about Jenkins's life. He was born on a plantation in South Carolina on February 6, 1880, four years after Eva's father was born in a shtetl in Nowogrod, Poland. Jenkins was educated at the Porter Military Academy in Charleston, South Carolina. He studied law and was admitted to the Bar of South Carolina in 1901 but did not practice. Seven years later he joined the Foreign Service as vice consul in Halifax, Nova Scotia. During the time he was serving in Hong Kong, Berlin, and Riga (Russia), Eva was born in Liverpool and attended the residential school for Jewish deaf children. Jenkins was consul general in London for only three years, from 1937 to 1939. Later he would be foreign minister to Bolivia, retiring in 1942 to live in Augusta, Georgia, where he availed himself of his hobbies, listed as "shooting and fishing." He died in 1961, eleven years before Eva did.

Jenkins had the sole task of deciding if Eva could go to the United States. But what a profound difference in world and life experience that would shape the fate of Eva and Morris (and me!). Jenkins's virtually aristocratic upbringing and his moving through the diplomatic elite as well as the power elite of the United States gave him no insight, one would assume, into the life of a Deaf, working-class, Jewish woman. His initial response to her application for a visa was to deny her the right to come to the United States, assuming that her poor background and deafness would lead her to become a charge of the state. And when she showed that her uncle was wealthy, perhaps wealthier than Jenkins, he thought someone must be lying. Only under the duress of documentation did Jenkins relent. Yet, despite his putting millstones around her neck, in Eva's description, we can almost feel a flirtatious admiration between the young Deaf woman and the world-weary diplomat. Their encounter was a minor moment in the history of the world—yet one in which power, authority, and gender sort themselves out and find their appointed places. Her working-class respect for those in power did not permit her to see Jenkins as an obstacle, an enemy, a man who could affect her future with a stroke of the pen. Instead, he was an object of fear and veneration. To him, she was a pretty, young deaf woman with whom he could joke about her marriage in a way that clearly would have been presumptuous with a woman of his own class. Did her race and her social position, along with her deafness, make her somewhat exotic to him? One can only speculate.

The letters that follow are the only ones that I have been able to locate. In editing them, I took care to change or omit almost nothing since I regard the letters as historical documents. I have added information in brackets where necessary and have refrained from correcting spelling and grammatical errors. Since I have decided to present the letters as they are, "warts and all," readers may be surprised to see a phrase like "I am as black as a niggar." While I surely recognize that most readers will find such a phrase offensive, I did not feel that I had the right to censor a historical document. My apologies for the insensitivity inherent in any such phrase.

I would like to thank John Vickrey Van Cleve and Ivey Pittle Wallace for their help, advice, and encouragement in getting these letters into print. Also thanks to Jenelle Walthour who ably edited the text. I would also like to appreciate Arlene Malinowski and Sam Parker for the brilliant dramatic interpretation of some of these letters that they performed at the 1998 CODA conference in Alexandria, Virginia. Arlene and Sam became Eva and Morris in a way I am unlikely ever to forget. Finally, I would like to thank Morris, whose pack-rat nature made it easy for him to hoard these letters so that we could all appreciate them, and my brother, Gerald, whose help in this project brought us closer together and brought him back into touch with deafness.

"I Shall Not Rush into Things…"

August 25, 1936 to November 3, 1937

*Eva sent this photograph to Morris shortly after
she sent him the letter dated 25/8/36.*

83 Chatham St.
Liverpool 7
25/8/36

Dear Morris,

It was indeed a surprise for me to receive your card & I shall say a pleasant surprise too.

I am sorry that I have not got a photo of myself at the present moment, but as soon as I have one I will send it to you.

Last Sunday I went to Hailbi Island with a deaf crowd which included Max, Leah & the Rubins. I am sure you would not recognize me now as I am as black as a niggar. I will probably go to Blackpool this Saturday for a day if the weather keeps good.

If ever you wish to come to Liverpool on a day's excursion you can be assured of a warm welcome. Max & Leah Purcell reciprocate your regards.

Yours sincerely,
Eva

לשנה טובה תכתבו.

With Sincere Good Wishes
.   for a   .
Bright and Happy New Year
And well over the Fast.
From Eva Weintrobe.

83, Chatham Street,
Liverpool, 7   1936-5697

This greeting card for the Jewish New Year was enclosed
with the following letter.

83 Chatham St.
Liverpool 7
24/9/36

Dear Morris,

Thanks for your letter which I was pleased to receive. It was a coincidence that you received the letter on your birthday, as I did not know. I hope I am not too late now to wish you the very best.

I noticed from your letter that all your family seem to have America in their blood, which reminds me, when do you intend going back? What are you doing with yourself these days? Are you working? Don't think I am very inquisitive. I have been very busy lately helping with the preparations for Yomtov [the holiday]. Anyway I am glad it is all over now & I am having a well earned rest.

I went the other day to see "Clark Gable" in "Mutiny on the Bounty". It is a picture worth seeing.

I will conclude now, wishing you well over the fast.

Sincerely,
Eva

83 Chatham St.
Liverpool 7
4/10/36

Dear Morris,

    I was pleased to receive your letter last week & to read that you are keeping well, as the same applies to myself.

    What made you think that I was sore with you about something. You can rest assure that I have nothing against you. If it was because I did not answer your letter sooner I want you to know that I am not a person of leisure & have not much time for letter writing.

    I am going to learn skating, an attempt to reduce my somewhat of late-increasing hips—Phew!

    Yes, I fasted well, in fact did not feel it much.

    I am at a loss to know what to write, this is unusual for me, but I have not the writing spell about me to-day.

    With kindest regards

> Sincerely,
> Eva.

83 Chatham St.
Liverpool 7
4/2/37

Dear Morris,

I shall be pleased to see you here on Saturday, but as I may be working on that day I cannot make any definite arrangements. I will do so with Annie Rubin to-morrow night. I am afraid Max & Leah will not be here as they are going to a Carnival at the Warrington Deaf Club.

With kindest regards to Molly & Hyman, & yourself

Your's
Eva Weintrobe

Eva (right) with Max (left) and Leah Purcell (second from left).

Invitation to the Warrington Deaf Club Social Tea Party, which Eva and Morris may have attended.

83 Chatham St.
Liverpool 7
10/3/37

Dear Morris,

I was very pleased to receive your letter yesterday. Yes, I enjoyed myself at Warrington in your company. I arrived home at about 12.30, not so bad.

I would have preferred you to come here on Saturday, but as I am working on that day, we will make it Sunday. I have told Max & Leah that you are coming. They have invited us over to their house in the evening. I will be at the station at 12.25. P.M. as you say in your letter.

I will keep the rest of the news until I see you on Sunday.

With kindest regards,

Your's Sincerely,
Eva

83 Chatham St.
Liverpool 7
18/3/37

Dear Morris,

I was pleased to receive your welcome letter. I am glad to say that I have now got rid of my cold.

I shall be at Lime St Station on Saturday night as I think it would be better than meeting at Lewis's.

As regards your intended visit we will speak about it when I see you. I'm afraid it will be difficult to be together at Sedar nights. It would be best if you come Sunday and Monday.

This notepaper is from a prize I won at the Deaf Club last night. Quite a handy prize.

With kindest regards from my family & myself.

Yours sincerely,
Eva

83 Chatham St.
Liverpool 7
24/3/37

Dear Morris,

I was pleased to receive your welcome letter. You have solved a problem about our mothers corresponding. I think it is a very good idea. We will speak about it when I see you.

I am looking forward to seeing you here on Sunday. Come as early as you can & don't lose your way.

I am afraid I will have to make this letter brief, as I am busy helping with the preparations for Pesach [Passover].

With kindest regards,

Your's sincerely,
Eva

83 Chatham St.
Liverpool 7
31/3/37

Dear Morris,

Many thanks for your very welcome letter which I
received today.

Why of course I am looking forward to seeing you on
Sunday, what makes you think otherwise?

Now Morris, how do you get the idea that I am playing with you. I can assure you that I have never felt the same
towards anyone else as I do towards you. The only thing
that is making me draw back is because everything seems so
strange getting married in such a rush, & going off to America
within only such a short time of knowing one another. Things
seldom happen like that these days.

I have been thinking hard since you went back & I
have come to the decision that the best thing for us to do is to
become engaged, surely if you love me as much as, I think you
do, this should not be too hard for you to do, after all twelve
months is nothing compared with ones whole life, in the meantime I could be preparing things.

I don't like the idea of getting married & waiting a year
before settling down. Every girl likes to have her own home
from the very first. If you want to save money as you said, but
which I do not care for, you can save more if you go alone.
After all many people wait longer than a year.

My father has written to one of my aunts in Brooklyn to visit your father.

Kindest regards from my family & my best love to you.

Sincerely,
Eva

83 Chatham St.
Liverpool 7
7/4/37

Dear Morris,

I received your welcome letter & was pleased to read that you are keeping well as I can say the same of myself.

We received a very nice letter from your sister to-day informing us that she will be pleased to see mother & myself on Sunday. I am looking forward to the trip.

I was talking the other day to one of the girls from our shop, without mentioning whom it concerns about immigrations as she has travelled a bit & understands these things. She told me that an American citizen does not have to go back to America to get a permanent stay in England but to apply at the Home Office here. America do[es] not care what you do, it is whether England permits you to stay. She also pointed out that it is not always that a wife is allowed into the States with her husband.

The thing that is puzzling me is this. How can you make money in one year as you say if you have been in the States twelve years & made nothing.

I would not like to get married unless you had a steady job. Even if we do go to America who knows if you would be able to obtain a job when we come back, you may not be so lucky as now & you know what this all leads to.

How do you expect me to get married in two months

time, it would be far too much of a rush for me. I would like
to get engaged first & get married a few months later. My
brother & sister both got engaged before they got married &
I would also like to get engaged first.

I hope I have made myself very clear, & I would like
you to understand Morris, that all this controversy is about
one thing & that is if only you would either remain in England
or go yourself to America, when I shall be prepared to get married as soon as you come back.

Kindest regards from my family & my best love to you.

Yours

Eva

P.S. Please give my regards to Molly and her husband.

Morris's sister, Jane, and his mother, Bella.

*Jane and
her husband, Harry.*

83 Chatham St.
Liverpool 7
12/4/37

Dear Morris,

Just a few lines to let you know that we arrived safely in Lime St at 5.20 A.M. after quite a comfortable journey.

I felt refreshed after a few hours sleep at home & went to work this afternoon. I had to make some excuse about being off in the morning, so I told them that I did not feel well & could not sleep the night before, which was partly true, they sent me to the Staff Welfare & took my temperature. I had to act the part & I think I did it well.

Please thank both Jane & your mother for the warm welcome they gave us. I hope it was not too much of a burden for Jane as I know she was not prepared for my brother coming.

I am not sorry that I went to London. I enjoyed every moment of my stay, mother too enjoyed herself & is none the worse for the trip.

I have not changed in my feelings toward you, but I am sorry that we have not come to a better understanding. Write to the Home Office as you promised, but first of all find out if you will be able to stay in England permanently. You would be making things easier for me, make both your & my mother content & prove to me that you really cared if you would agree to become engaged & go back to America for a few months, but if you are still determined to take me with you try to prolong your stay here for another few months.

How is Jane's husband I hope he is better now & Jane has got over the worry.

When are you coming to Liverpool again? I hope it will be soon.

Kindest regards to your sister & mother from my mother & myself.

With best love,

Sincerely,
Eva

Rev. J. Weintrobe, B.A. [Eva's brother]
9, Willows Place,
Swansea,
South Wales
14/4/37

Dear Mrs. Folus [Morris's sister]:

I arrived home at 4 o'clock on Monday afternoon. I found everyone well, T[hank]. G[od]. I do hope your husband is quite well again.

I am very glad to have met you and the other members of your family. I hope to have the pleasure of meeting you on many more occasions.

The lawyer, from whom I wished to inquire re the possibility of Morris being able to stay in England for good, is at present away—I shall not be able to see him till the week-end. I should like to know what reply Morris receives from the Home Office.

Kindest regards from my wife & myself to your mother, Morris, your husband & yourself.

Yours Sincerely,
Joseph Weintrobe

*Eva's brother, Rabbi Joseph Weintrobe,
in his military chaplain uniform.*

Any communication on the
subject of this letter should be
addressed to:—   Home Office,
The Under Secretary of State   Whitehall.
Aliens Department   17th April, 1937
Home Office
London, S.W. 1
and the following number quoted: D.2951

The Under Secretary of State is directed to return the passport of Mr. Morris Davis in which the following endorsement has been made:

"The condition attached to the grant of leave to land is hereby varied so as to require that the holder:

(i) Does not remain in the United Kingdom longer than 28th July, 1937.

(ii) Does not enter any employment paid or unpaid, while in the United Kingdom."

The endorsement in the passport must be shown at once to the Police Registration Officer of the registration district in which the holder is resident.

The matter of Mr. Davis' return from the United States of America cannot be decided in advance. It will be open to him to apply to the nearest Passport Control Officer or British Consul for a visa. If Mr. Davis desires to return for the purpose of employment, he should first be in possession of a permit issued to his prospective employer by the Minister of Labor.

Mr. Davis' certificate of registration is also returned herewith.

Mr. M. Davis,
c/o Mrs. J. Folus,
38, Parfett Street,
E. 1

83 Chatham St.
Liverpool 7
18/4/37

Dear Morris,

Many thanks for your welcome letter, was glad to read that you have now settled down in your own home.

I had a nice letter from my brother Joe. He wrote that he was pleased to meet you & he spoke very nice about you.

We have been very busy working overtime the last few nights dispite the fact that we have had a lot of temporary helpers in lately &, with my own private orders, I have not had much spare time to write earlier.

After all this fuss I see no excitement at the prospect of going to America even for a short stay. I am *pleading* with you to either stay in England or go back alone for a few months, nothing will be too hard for you, if you know that I shall be waiting for you. Why don't you act like other boys & give in to the girl. Many would sacrifice much more than this. I am begging you to listen to my plead. Even your own mother & sister have said it would be better for you to stay in England.

I am glad that you have agreed to get engaged first, as it is the proper thing for us to do, but I would be happier if you bought it with me & as there is no immediate hurry I can wait until it is possible for you to get it.

I am beginning to miss your Sundays here & am looking forward to your next visit. I am enclosing a photo as I promised, it is only a cheap one & not very good. I will have a better one taken when I have the time.

My people send their kindest regards to your family & yourself.

I close with my best love to you,

Your's Sincerely,
Eva

83 Chatham St.
Liverpool 7
21/4/37

Dear Morris,

I received your welcome letter this morning. I am sorry that you were worried last week about my letter but as I explained everything there is no need for me to do so again. You can see that I am answering this straight away so that you will be in no suspense again.

Morris, you are not being fair to me & are looking at things from a different point of view, sometimes I wonder whether you really care for me. You said I should not doubt your love for me as you were the first to declare & also the first to propose marriage, well this is the proper thing to do, did you expect me to propose first.

You said that your girl friends have said that they would follow their husband's anywhere, don't forget that I said the same at first thought, but if they were in the position that I am now I know that they would say differently. I don't care in what part of England you choose to live, I would go with you, but to live in America so far away. Even Janie said that if Eddie had asked her to go to America she would have thought twice as much. Max Purcell has always wanted to go to South Africa, but his wife will never consent to going, & he has given in to her.

I know that I am wasting time, but I cannot give a definite answer until I get a letter from my Auntie in America.

If I do give in & go with you, I do not want to live with a father-in-law & look after him, you are expecting too much of me. I don't like the attitude he took concerning our affair & it makes me wonder if I will be able to get on with him. I don't blame Eddie [Jane's husband] in telling Jane to ask your mother to lessen her frequent calls as he did not want her advices. I too would never ask you to take advice of my mother once we were married.

I don't understand what you mean by your mother agreeing to your fathers opinion & your decision as she would like to see you happy, to what decision are you referring?

You have no right to balance my love for you in whether I go to America with you or not.

I shall be very pleased to see you here on May 2nd & I hope by that time we shall have cleared something up & come to a better understanding.

We are expecting my sister-in-law from Swansea [Joe's wife Rose] & the baby [Elkan] here for a few weeks stay shortly. It is a long time since we last saw them.

I will close with my best love to you.

Your's sincerely,
Eva

83 Chatham St.
Liverpool 7
26/4/37

Dear Morris,

Many thanks for your welcome letter which I received on Saturday. Yes, come down next Sunday May 2nd. I will be very pleased to see you. We shall be expecting a large company here on that day. My sister-in-law [Rose] is going to Manchester this week to stay with her mother for a short holiday, & will be here on Sunday, & I think my brother Joe will be coming too. A member of his congregation who was formerly from Liverpool is coming over by car to unveil a stone for her father's grave & asked my brother to accompany them. Max [Eva's brother] I believe will be getting engaged on that day. His girl is here at the present moment.

We had a letter from my Auntie in America. She wrote that she had been to see your father & he gave her a good impression of you. Your father also told her that there may be difficulty in getting me into the States. So you see we must look at every small thing. You may not be permitted to stay in England, what could we do then. I have told you before that I would never agree to get married & then you go to America alone. It is allright for cricketers & film stars, Jewish people never do things like this.

Let me know what time you will arrive here next Sunday & at what station. I am not sure but I think there will be an affair at Max's girls house on Sunday.

How are your family getting on, please give them my best regards.

With best love,

Your's
Eva

83 Chatham St.
Liverpool 7
5/5/37

Dear Morris,

I was pleased to receive your welcome letter & read that you had a comfortable journey home. I was wondering all the time if you had got a good seat.

Don't stop your mother if she wants to write to my father or better still she can write to my brother the address is 9, Willows Place, Swansea, South Wales. I let my parents go to any length as I know they were only doing it for my own benefit.

I had a long talk with my brothers on Sunday night & they told me that no one in the family will stand in the way of my happiness & the best conclusion at which they can arrive is that you go back to America when your visa expires. I should follow later, as I cannot go away before Max's wedding in August or September. Meanwhile they will make arrangements for me to stay with my Aunt. Then I can judge how I like America & I can then decide on staying & marrying you or returning. It is best to make sure of things first, once you are married nothing can ever alter matters.

We are still working overtime & to-day Wednesday we have been working until four o'clock instead of one. I shall be glad when all this rush is over.

Kindest regards from all my family & my best love to you.

Your's Sincerely,
Eva

Rev. J. Weintrobe
9, Willows Place,
Swansea,
South Wales
7.5.37

Dear Mrs. Folus [Morris's sister],

I hope that your husband, mother, Morris & yourself are keeping well. My wife & the baby are at present in Manchester on a short visit to my mother-in-law. My father is staying with me. He has not been very well, & is having a little holiday here.

Morris has, no doubt, told you about his visit on Sunday last to Liverpool. It is a great pity that things are not going so smoothly. I should very much like Morris to adopt a more reasonable attitude. The following suggestion, which, I believe, Eva has already made, should be satisfactory. It is that Morris should go to America when his visa expires. Eva will follow soon after my brother [Max] is married, which we expect him to be in August. Eva would have about 6 months in America to see how she would like the country, how she would like being away from home, & how she & Morris would get on when they would be on their own, away from family influences. Morris could in the meantime establish himself, if possible, in a good post. Then, if mutually agreeable, they could live in America, after getting married there. It is because of the uncertainty of it all that we do not wish them to marry here, & then chance it in America. But, if Morris will be reasonable, Eva will follow him, she would probably stay with an aunt of ours, & then, as I said, they could follow this up & get married. This would solve the difficulty, if Morris would be agreeable, & I think he ought to be prepared to do this, if he cared sufficiently.

I had been hoping to be in London, but I have not yet been able to get away.

Kind regards to you all from my father & myself.

Yours Sincerely,
Joseph Weintrobe

[In the corner of the letter, Morris wrote: "Please return it to me, Morris." He apparently sent the letter to Eva to read.]

This may be the photograph of Morris to which Eva refers in the next letter.

83 Chatham St.
Liverpool 7
9/5/37

Dear Morris,

Many thanks for your most welcome letter received yesterday. I would very much like to see you before you go back to America, but I would prefer you come to Liverpool, as this is the busiest time of the year at our workshop & I could not possibly get off the next day, as I did last time & with working overtime most nights it would be too much of a strain.

I am glad that we have come to a better understanding. Yes I foresaw all the possibility that Joe would not be officiating at the wedding & my family would not be there if we got married in America. It would hurt me more than I'd care to admit, but I think it is for the best & so do my parents. [D]on't think they are saying this just to make us happy as you said in your letter, they are not the kind to play with me. I never said when I will go to America I just mentioned I cannot leave before Max's wedding in Sept., but Morris I want you to understand that if ever I change my mind & do not want to go don't blame me, it would be partly your fault as you are very obstinate, if you are vexed with me for saying this I am very sorry, but I want to be frank with you, & tell you just what I think.

It is hard for me to make things plainer to you what I wrote in the last letter. I mean that I am taking a very big risk in going away & want to make sure first that everything will be alright, so that I will not be sorry after. I know you do not mean to stay for good, still one never knows what will happen.

I think your first photo was better.

I will close now hoping to see you soon here.

> With best love,
> Eva

PS: If you read the Jewish Chronicle you will see Max's engagement announced.

83 Chatham St.
Liverpool 7
11/5/37

Dear Morris,

I received your welcome letter to-day. I do not feel any bitterness towards you if that is what you think. Your letter has put me in an awkward position. Although we have discussed this several times, I still do not understand, you say if I married you, you would come back to England soon, yet knowing that I would be waiting for you does not make you want to hurry back. Yes, Max will be getting married only three months after being engaged but you forget that he has known Doris for a long time.

You imag[in]e for some reason or other that I am vexed or dissatisfied with you, it is the attitude you are taking which is making you imagine these things.

As much as I would like you to come here for a whole week it would be us[e]less. As you know that father is in Swansea, Mother has to take his place & stay with Betty in the shop all day & you would be alone & then again I am working overtime most nights & would not be able to see much of you. You could come here for a day on Sunday.

Morris please do not let any ill feelings mar our friendship. If you are still agreeable to my suggestion of last week, we will keep to that plan & I shall be looking forward to seeing you again soon.

Morris (second from left) in a walking race in England.

Let me congratulate you on winning in the Road Walking championship last week & I wish you the best of luck for your next one.

Kindest regards from my family. I close with my best love to you,

Yours Sincerely,
Eva

Eva's uncles and aunts at the Concord Hotel in the early 1950s. Her father, Eli, is standing second from the right. Her Aunt Molly Harrison is seated at the far left. Arthur Winarick, married to Eva's Aunt Jean (seated fourth from the right), is standing third from the right.

83 Chatham St.
Liverpool 7
26/5/97

Dear Morris,

Just a few hurried lines so that you will get this letter to-morrow before going to the Shipping Office. I went to Celia's [Eva's sister] straight from work this afternoon & have only just come home & found your letter, so I am writing without delay to catch the last post.

Nothing will make me change my mind. I have told you before that I will not rush into things. It is impossible for me to marry you in July.

I will send you the address of my Auntie in America in my next letter. I believe it was a lovely day in London on Sunday. We are still having rain here. It seems that once it starts it is a long time stopping.

Kindest regards from my family to your mother, sister & yourself.

With best love,

Yours Sincerely,
Eva

83 Chatham St.
Liverpool 7
30/5/37

Dear Morris,

I was pleased to receive your welcome letter yesterday. In your previous letter to me you asked me to reply without delay as you had to go to the Home Office to either verify or cancel your passage to America & it all depended on my answer. So I naturally gave you a curt reply so that you would know what to do & as I had explained to you that I was in a hurry I thought that you would understand. Of course I will miss you & shall be sorry when you go back. I shall be looking forward to the day when I will be able to see you again.

I was thinking of seeing you off at Southampton on Wednesday, but I find that it is impossible to get off from work. Two girls are away ill & a few have taken their holiday now, otherwise I would have gone, as I had wanted see you off. You wrote in your letter that you were miserable, what is it about, cheer up, & look on the bright side of things & everything will be allright.

Please convey to Norman [Jackson, Morris's friend] my congratulations on his coming marriage [to Lily] & my best wishes for a bright & happy future.

We are having lovely weather now & about time. Mother is going to Swansea next week & I hope that the rest will do her good.

I will close now wishing you a Bon Voyage.
With my best love to you,

> Your's very Sincerely,
> Eva

PS Write & let me know how you like the "Queen Mary"

83, Chatham St.,
Liverpool 7.
June 1st

Dear Morris,

I received your welcome letter this morning before going to work & am answering during lunch hour. As much as I would like to see you off at Southampton I am afraid it is impossible. As with less girls here we have to make up for lost time, & may be working until 4 o'clock to-morrow (Wednesday).
Wishing you once more a "bon voyage" Love. Eva.

A letter from Eva to Morris, June 1, 1937.

83 Chatham St.
Liverpool 7
June 1st

Dear Morris,

I received your welcome letter this morning before going to work & am answering during lunch hour. As much as I would like to see you off at Southampton I am afraid it is impossible. As with less girls here we have to make up for lost time, & may be working until 4 o'clock to-morrow/Wednesday.

Wishing you once more a "bon voyage"

Love.
Eva.

Annie and Ada Rubin.

83 Chatham St.
Liverpool 7
20/6/37

Dear Morris,

I was very pleased to receive your welcome letter &
card. I received both at the same time although I noticed that
the card was sent earlier. You honured me by writing your first
letter in America to me.

I met Leah the other day & she told me that she had
received a card from you. She is moving soon taking a half
house with her mother & father. Harold [Celia's son] also
showed me a card from you.

Mother has been in Swansea two weeks & is staying
another two. I hope the rest will do her good. Now we girls
have the opportunity to learn cooking. I think Betty is the better of the two of us. I am thinking of going away for my holiday with Ada Rubin. Annie is going to Paris for the Deaf
Congress. We are probably going to Rhyl. It is a very nice
place with plenty of amusements. We are going there today
to look for rooms.

We are still very busy at work & working late some
nights. It seems that people are mad on clothes this year. Have
you got your old job back? Last Sunday we went hiking in
North Wales taking the train halfway. There were eight of us
including Max Leah & the Rubins.

Do you remember me showing you some snaps of my

cousins in America one specially of two girls & the mother. Well one of them is getting married this week.

I am enclosing the address of my Auntie. You could go & visit her & give her a regard from us. We had a letter from her the other day asking if I am going to the States.

How is Norman [Jackson] is he married yet.

I will close now hoping to hear from you soon.

With best love & shall I say a kiss

Yours Sincerely,
Eva

Mrs. S. Weintraub
681 Hawthorne St
Brooklyn N.Y.

83 Chatham St.
Liverpool 7
21/7/37

Dear Morris,

I was very pleased to receive your much looked forward to letter. I also received the parcel & thank you very much for same. Harold was delighted at the Comics[.] You should have seen his face when he saw them. After I mailed my last letter to you I received the other parcel you sent from the ship. Harold was also very pleased with the novelties. I enjoyed reading the papers as I always find American newspapers very interesting[.]

Yes it does seem an enternity in receiving your letter after being used to receiving them every week when you were in England[.] You asked me to write longer letters[.] I will try my best, but I have told you before that I am not a very good letter writer & you must not forget that I do not have very much time to spare. There is always sewing laying about for me to do which reminds me that I will have to start with my holiday cloths as I am going away in two weeks time, there I am going on when I suppose you are not interested. You asked me again why I do not write more sentimental & intimate letters. I am not a poet & cannot express my feelings in black & white & feel I will not be doing justice to my feelings.

Max's engagement I am sorry to say has come to an end. It is no good for you to ask me the why's & wherefor's[.]

[T]he only satisfactory answer I can give you is that Max was not very happy over the engagement & thought it best to finish before it is too late. Of course we are very upset as it seemed a good chance for Max & we were hoping things would turn out well[.]

You ask me what my plans for the future are[.] I must confess I have made none. I miss you very much, but I am happy & content here. Just as you say, you are wrestling with the problem of what is best to do so am I[.] I do not know which way to turn. We had a letter from Auntie Sarah & she wrote that she will do all she can for me if I decide to go to America. Father wrote a long letter telling her everything & I wrote a few lines thanking her for the trouble she has taken[.] I suppose she will be inviting you down again soon.

Harold is not having his operation after all, Celia does not think it necessary. They are at present in Dublin with Jack's sister for a few weeks holiday. We miss them very much.

I suppose you heard when you were in Manchester that Molly Alper's brother-in-law was engaged to a Liverpool girl. I believe they will be getting married in August, so I suppose the crowd will be coming down. I don't think I will be able to see them as I think the Wedding will take place when I am on my holiday.

I have taken up tennis once again & hope to play more regular. I play every Friday evening with some friends from the Deaf Club.

Morris, what do you do with yourself now[,] are you back again with your old friends? The other day Annie & Ada

Rubin & Leah & Max asked me about you & if I had heard from you & I told them I had without telling everything.

I started writing this letter last night but was too tired to finish it so am writing now before going to work. I hope you are keeping well as I am glad to say the same of myself.

Kindest regards from my family
With best love & kisses

Your's
Eva

Celia, Eva's sister, with her husband, Jack Ross, and their son, Harold.

SCHOOL DAYS

1938

Harold, Eva's nephew, a year after his accident.

83 Chatham St.
Liverpool 7
Aug 22nd

Dear Morris,

Very many thanks for your eagerly awaited letter. I also thank you very much for the birthday present, it was an unexpected but pleasant surprise & I shall buy something useful as you advised with the money.

I am feeling fine after my holiday at Rhyl & I had a very enjoyable time, the weather too was fine the whole time. I am not sure if you would recognize me now as I am nearly as black as a niggar. We went swimming everyday & sight seeing now & again. Esther Tanen & her husband were in Manchester for a week & took the opportunity of spending a day with us. They talked quite a bit about you but nothing serious. I am enclosing a few snaps.

When Celia was in Dublin she met Jack's cousin a hearing girl & her deaf husband, they have not been married long. [T]he boy Harold Rosenberg, he is not from our school, told my sister that his family all went to America & have been trying for the last few years to get him over but cannot because he is deaf. They had been doing all that was in their power to do. I have a feeling that there will be uncertainty in getting me over. Things are not the same as when you first went to America.

Although I would like to have the engagement ring for my birthday [September 3] owing to all this uncertainty, I think it would be much wiser to wait until something definite is settled.

Have you been to Auntie Sarah's again? [I]f so, let me know what happened there.

I have not been to the Shipping Offices as I really do not know what to do, in a way I would like to go to America but in another way I think it would be better for me to remain in England, don't think it is the family's fault as it is not, father for instance is urging me to go[.] Mother I must admit does not like the idea[.] [S]till she is not standing in the way. Don't think that all this is because I have changed towards you, as it is not true. I care for you just the same as when you were in England. I miss you & also the good times we had together when you were here.

Harold had an accident with his hand[.] [H]e slipped on the moving stairs at Lewis's & caught his hand in a small hole, but luckily there was no machinery working at the time, otherwise it would have been worse, as it is he has only a few bruises & cuts. He goes to school now & talks about nothing else all day. Isaac Butnick passed away a few weeks ago, it must be a great loss to the family, as he was still only a young man. I believe he had been poorly for some time.

How are you keeping & how is your father? I thank him for the trouble he had taken in going to the Shipping Office for the affidavits.

There is really nothing in the way of news to write about, so I will close wishing you a Happy New Year.

With best love & kisses to you,

> Yours Sincerely
> Eva

PS
I started writing this letter on Sunday but had to wait until
today for the snaps. E.

לשנה טובה תכתבו ותחתמו

⁂.

5698-1937

Miss Eva Weintrobe
Sincerely wishes you
A Happy and Prosperous New Year
and Well over the Fast.

83, Chatham Street,
Liverpool, 7.

Eva sent this New Year's card with her letter of 22/8/37.

83 Chatham St.
Liverpool 7
25/8/37

Dear Morris,

After receiving your letters & affidavits this morning, I have now decided that I will go to America, if all is well. Max [Eva's brother] is away at the present, but will be home this weekend & I will then ask him to come with me to the American Consul as he understands these things better than I do. I am happy & excited at the prospect of seeing you again & I hope you will not have long to wait. I will let you know all as soon as I have been to the Consul. I will ask for a permanent visa as you advised.

I feel now after receiving your letters that I will be safe in America, whereas before I received them I had felt some uncertainty, now I know everything will be alright.

I am glad that my Aunties gave you a warm welcome.

I will write again next week & will let you know all. Hoping it will not be long before I go to America.

With best love & kisses to you

Yours
Eva

83 Chatham St.
Liverpool 7
19/9/37

Dear Morris,

Very many thanks for your ever welcome letter received. Since writing my last letter to you I have been going on with the affair. I went to the American Consulate here, but was told to apply to the Consulate General in London, as they only give Visitor's Visas here. I wrote to London & sent the affidavits & received an enquiry form. I have also sent this back & yesterday I received a letter for an interview on Oct 12th & was told in the meantime to get all the necessary papers ready. It is rather a long time to wait, but I suppose I cannot rush them. The appointment is for 10:30 A.M. I am going to write & ask them to make it for 3:30 as I will probably travel on that day [to London from Liverpool]. I will write to your sister Janie & will tell her everything.

I received the affidavits from my four Uncles. I was surprised to receive the one from my Uncle Arthur [Winarick] the maker of Jeris preparations. Did you see him or did Auntie Sarah ask him to fill them in.

What made you think it is through your money that decided me to go to America. I told you before that I don't care if you have not a penny. It was the letter from your bosses that decided me, do you remember when you were here that I asked you if you were sure of getting your job back, you said yes of course, & I told you not to be too sure. You must admit it would have been silly of me, if you had not been working & I went over to join you, other bosses would have put another in your place no matter what a good worker you were if you had been away so long. I think you are very lucky to get your old job back.

Father should not have told Auntie about your financial affairs & I told him so. It was not from the letter from your Banker that he saw it, it was from the affidavits & I did not think he would attract any attention to it. To come to think of it I wish you had not mentioned anything about your financial affairs still what has been done cannot be undone & you have nothing to be ashamed of. If my relations want to help me they can do so without thinking of what you have. Don't forget that what father did was solely for my welfare.

You need not worry about asking anybody to lend me a wedding dress. I have been working hard & will not go to America empty handed so will be able to buy my own dress.

There is one thing I cannot agree about the engagement ring. It is not right for a girl to buy the ring & put it on herself. You can buy the ring immediately [when] I arrive in America if you wish.

You have no need to worry, I will be a good wife to you, & will do everything for you as long as you are good to me. I am going to give up a lot for you leaving all my family & friends, so this ought to prove something to you.

Mrs. Alberts & her sister Mrs. Corkland, you remember spending the night at their house last Pesach, have just left

Liverpool & are now living in Birmingham. I was busy making things for them before they left. They asked me about you & wish to be remembered to you. I told them of my decision to go to America & they wished me luck & asked me to visit them before I leave England. I am keeping well hoping this letter finds you the same.

I suppose you are bored with this letter by now so I will close.

With best love & kisses
Eva

PS Please give my regards to your father, sister & brother.

83 Chatham St.
Liverpool 7
10/10/37

Dear Morris,

    Very many thanks for your ever welcome letter received last Friday. I also received the card you sent me from Massachasetts.

    You will notice by the above date that I am going to London next week to see the Consulate. I have already sent the affidavits on. I was told to bring a statement with me from someone of good standing who has known me for a number of years. My minister has very kindly done this for me & he has also given me some very good advice. If they will not let me land unless I marry you on the boat I would be prepared to, but I would much rather wait until I am in America & have a proper wedding. My minister said if you show them proof that you will marry me & I have some relations to go to in the meantime they will then let me land. It is proper and decent for Jewish people to get married in a synagogue.

    I think your idea about the ring is very good. As soon as I get my visa I will let you know. You can then send the money to Max & I will go with him to choose the ring. I would also like to have the engagement ring before I leave England. I hope everything will be alright for us both in the end.

    What made you think I get bored with your long letters when I am always looking eagerly forward to receiving them.

With very best wishes for a happy birthday. I know that I am a little late, but better late than never.

love

Nina.

TO WISH YOU
A VERY HAPPY BIRTHDAY

This card's my little mascot.

To wish you luck to-day.

A lot of joy, a little wealth.

The best of thrills, the best of health.

No matter where you stray.

It was only by a chance that I asked you if you were bored with mine.

I was down at Leah's last night, she has been ill for the last three weeks but is getting better now. They told me that they had received a letter from you & thank you for same. Joe also wrote that he had received your letter.

Celia [Eva's sister] has now moved & lives with Jack's father [Celia's father-in-law]. I cannot remember whether I told you or not that Jack's mother passed away a few weeks ago & as his sister is getting married soon it is very quite [quiet] for the old man, so he asked Jack & Celia to live with them [him?].In the middle of writing this letter Annie Rubin called. She asked me who I was writing to, so I told her, she sends her regards to you & also Ada's. She came to ask me if I would like to go to Chester as a friend of ours invited us over.

I was wondering why you had sent me three copy's of the affidavits whereas my Auntie sent two. If you like I can send the pink copy back in my next letter or I could keep it together with the other papers.

I am keeping well hoping this letter finds you the same.

I will close now with my best love to you. My family send their best regards to you.

Yours very Sincerely,
Eva

83 Chatham St.
Liverpool 7
14/10/37

Dear Morris,

I have come back from the Consulate very disappointed whereas I had gone with great hopes. This letter gives me no pleasure in writing as I had expected to write quite a different one. I went to London with Betty [Eva's sister] as the family thought it would be better for me & I was glad she came as she was some comfort to me.

I went to the Consulate at the appointed time, at first I went through the medical examination in this I easily passed so I thought there would be no difficulty in getting the Visa but in this I was very much disappointed. The Consulate asked me at first what I would do if you suddenly changed your mind & did not want to marry me. I told him that was impossible, & besides ever since leaving school I have always been self independent. I told him we could get married as soon as my ship lands, but he told me that he would only be doing me more harm than good if he gave me a visa as I would be deported which would not be nice. He said that the only thing to do is for you to come to England & marry me then nothing whatever will stand in the way of me going back with you as your wife, to show me proof of this he has given me back all the affidavits but kept yours & written on it, pending, expecting my return for the visa. I told him that it was impossible for you to come back as you had only gone back last June. He said he was sorry but that was the only thing to do.

The reason why he refused the visa is because he was afraid you would not marry me & then I would be destitute & be dependent on the city.

I had written to your sister Janie that I was coming but did not receive a reply[.] [T]hinking that she may have moved I wrote another addressed to your mother. I received an answer saying she would be pleased to see me. I told your mother everything, she was disappointed too, as she had thought I would get the visa.

There is nothing I can do now, it is for you to decide whether you care to come to England to marry me. I know this is a lot for you to do, still you can see it was not my fault, I did all I could.

I received your parcel this morning & thank you for same. I am too upset to write any more, so I will close hoping we will both find a way in the end.

With best love,

Yours very Sincerely,
Eva

U.S. Department of Labor
Immigration and Naturalization Service
Washington

October 29, 1937
Mr. Morris Davis
32 Meserole Street
Brooklyn, N.Y.

Dear Sir:

Reference is made to our attached letter of October 19, regarding your desire to secure the admission to the United States of your fiancée, Miss Eva Weintrobe. You state that the American Consul in London refused to issue a visa to her, that you are a United States citizen, and that you and she are deaf.

Inasmuch as your ultimate object is to secure your fiancée's permanent admission to the United States, it is suggested that efforts be continued to secure an immigration visa for her. Under the law the consuls, who are officials of the Department of State, have entire authority in the issuance of visas, and this office does not instruct the consuls. If you go abroad to marry, thereafter you make a petition for the granting of a nonquota status in the issuance of an immigration visa to your wife. The forms for this purpose may be secured from and executed before an American consul. However, approval of the visa petition is not an assurance that a visa will be issued, its only purpose being to accord the beneficiary an exempt status so far as the quota is concerned.

In case Miss Weintrobe desires to seek entry as a vistor to the United States, she should secure a passport visa from an American consul. An alien admitted as visitor after June 30, 1924, may not remain here permanently, notwithstanding marriage to a United States citizen. If your fiancée should be admitted as a visitor, in order to secure the right of permanent residence in the United States it will be necessary for her to leave the country, procure a proper immigration visa from an American consul in foreign territory, and thereafter undergo examination by officials of this Service at a United States port of entry.

As indicated above, decision in this case now rests with the American Consul at London, to whom your further inquiries and representations should be submitted. As of possible assistance, there is attached a pamphlet of general information regarding the United States immigration laws.

Cordially yours,
By direction of the
Commissioner,

Henry B. Hazard, Assistant

In Reply Refer to
File No. 811.11 - RWB/fh

The Foreign Service
of the
United States of America

American Consulate General
1, Grosvenor Square, London, W.1.
November 3, 1937

Miss Eva Weintrobe
83 Chatham Street
Liverpool 7.

Madam:

In regard to your desire to emigrate to the United
States, it is suggested that you send the enclosed Forms B to
your fiancé in the United States with the request that he and
your several aunts in that country comply carefully with all
the pertinent requirements, which are fully explained therein.

Whenever you have received the necessary additional
evidence from all of your relatives, please send it to this office
for examination. If it is found to be sufficient, the Consulate
General will be pleased to reconsider your application with
a view of granting the desired visa.

Very truly yours,
For the American Consul,

Russel W. Benton
American Vice Consul

Enclosures: Two Forms B.

83 Chatham St.
Liverpool 7
3/11/37

Dear Morris,

I received your letter this morning. I am surprised &
shocked with what you had written. You say that Betty & I
told your mother that my Uncle [Arthur Winarick] should
smooth matters out by paying your passage over. It is entirely
untrue, we would never dream of doing such a thing. Your
mother suggested to me that I should pay your fare over. I did
not like to say anything about this to you before, but as matters have gone a bit too far I am compelled to do so, what surprised me most is that you should fall to such a suggestion.
You have put my family in a very awkward position.

You did not even ask permission of me if you should
ask Uncle Arthur for help, even if you had I would never have
given my consent.

And another thing you have made me vexed with is
that you always make plans & arrangements without asking
the other concerned whether they like it or not.

Uncle Arthur may be a rich man but he has to work for
his living & he works hard. He has his own expenses & family
to think of.

I wonder what our relations think of us now.

This is all I can say for the present.

From
Eva

"Wondering...
If Your Love
Had Ever Been Deep"

November 11, 1937 to April 22, 1938

83 Chatham St.
Liverpool 7
11/11/37

Dear Morris,

I suppose you have already received my previous letter & the cablegram. I received your letter. There are some things I cannot understand about you. How in the world could you expect me to be prepared to marry you & sail to America in three weeks time. I have been thinking things over & I have come to the conclusion that it is better for us to end things now. I am very very sorry that things have gone so far, but you never ask my opinion on anything that you make your mind up, it seems to me that when you make up your mind on a subject you do not ask anyone's opinion.

I hope that I have not hurt you too much. I myself find it very hard to write this letter, but I think it is for the best. I shall always remember you as a very good friend.

I will close wishing you the best of luck & I hope you will some day find the happiness you crave.

Eva

83 Chatham St.
Liverpool 7
22/11/37

Dear Morris,

I received your welcome letter & thank you for same. I am very sorry that I had hurt you with my letters, but you see I was very vexed with what you had written first about asking my Uncle Arthur for help & then rushing me with the wedding. I answered right away without thinking how much the letter would hurt you & I humbly apologise for all that I had said. I wish you would in future let me know beforehand what you intend doing so that things would run more smoothly.

I wrote to your mother & told her about the cablegram I had sent you, so that she would not be expecting you.

I am glad that you enjoyed yourself at Uncle Arthur's. I suppose you told them everything, as I received the cable from Auntie Jean [Arthur's wife].

I shall be waiting to hear what you have to say.

With kindest regards

Your's Sincerely,
Eva

83 Chatham St.
Liverpool 7
16-12-37

Dear Morris,

I was very pleased to receive your very welcome letter. I am glad that the misunderstanding between us has cleared up & I hope things will now run more smoothly. I know that I had been too hasty in sending that letter to Auntie Jean, but you cannot deny that at your first visit to the Winaricks had been for the sole purpose of asking them to help you. I was afraid that you would have asked before she received my letter & I did not want her to think our family would stoop so low. When I was in London with you I remember your sister telling me that when you said a thing you mean it, & you also wrote that you were not afraid to ask them to help you. You should have told Auntie Jean at the very first why I was vexed with you, as I also feel very embarrassed now that Auntie showed you my letter to her. The reason I sent the other letter ending things between us was because I was frantic with worry first with your intentions of asking Uncle for help & then with your hasty plans of coming to England, so you can see that I am not fully to blame.

I had a letter from the Consulate but it seems that you did not explain that I had previously applied for a visa as he instructed me to send papers to you for affidavits & letters from your bank & place of employment. I am afraid it is useless to write to the Consulate as it is very hard to make them change.

Max is engaged to a very nice girl from Tredgar South Wales. The wedding will take place soon.

The Jewish Club in London are having a Carnival in January & they have asked me if I would like to go. I am not sure yet whether to go as it means travelling home in the night & I had enough of it when I went to London to visit the Consulate. By the way, I forgot to tell you that Beatie Socolove is coming over this Saturday & has asked me to go to the Club as she is dying to see me, wonder if it is true, we have not met since leaving school.

With kindest regards from all

Love Eva

83 Chatham St.
Liverpool 7
8/2/38

Dear Morris,

I received your letter & the parcel of papers for which I thank you. Harold was here when it came & he was very delighted with the comics. He refused to eat his dinner saying he was too busy.

Yes, I received your letter of Dec. 24th. I had been putting of[f] answering it, as I have realised since receiving the letter, that I do not want to go out to America, as I hate to hurt your feelings I have delayed in answering, but I know that I have no right to keep you in suspense. It would be useless you coming over here in March, as I know nothing will make me change. I am very sorry Morris, but I think it is for the best for the both of us. I suppose it would be useless for us to carry on in this way.

I will always remember you as a very good friend & send you my best wishes for the future,

Eva

83 Chatham St.
Liverpool 7
23/3/38

Dear Morris,

I do not know how to start this letter but first of all I
will humbly apologise for the way I have treated you. I have
made a big mistake[.] [A]t first I was too proud to admit it, but
I now realise that it is best to put pride aside to achieve ones
happiness. The trouble all started through this, one of the girls
from our Club went to Leeds & saw Isadore Alper, he asked
her for my address & started writing to me, he knew from the
beginning that I was corresponding with you. Molly must
have told him and begged me to stop writing to you, the family persuaded me that it was better for me to be married to a
boy residing in England, so that was why I sent you the last
letter, but as soon as I had done so I realised that I had made
a big mistake & that I would not be happy with another boy
& that you were the only one[.] [A]s I said before I was too
proud to admit it, the family can now see that they too had
made a mistake in encouraging me to have the Leeds boy.
Morris I am very sorry for all the trouble I have caused you
& hope to make up for it when we are together again if you
can find it in you to forgive. I have done nothing wrong to
be ashamed of[.] [I]t is only that I thought it would be better
what the family said & I now fully realise my mistake. Auntie
Jean is quite right in saying girls are very chang[e]able.

The sooner we get married the better it will be to save any more misunderstanding which may arise. I have been thinking that it would be better for me to apply for a visitor's visa & then stay in America[.] [I]n this way I would be able to go sooner, where as if I applied for a permanent visa I may again be refused as I had Uncles affidavit with me when I went last Oct. & it did not seem to impress the Consulate. If you still think I should apply for a permanent visa would you please write to your sister Janie & ask her to go to the Consulate & explain things for me, to mention that I had previously applied for one & had been refused through my deafness[.] [I]n this way she will be saving me a lot of trouble. I went through enough of it when I was down last October. Or if you wish you can come to England & I will be prepared to marry you any time.

Max is getting married the 1st of May, his girl [Ann] was down here some time ago & we all took a great liking to her. She comes of a very nice family[,] one of her brothers is a Minister in Margate & the other an author. I am very busy making the dresses for the wedding. I have also made a few frocks for Ann (Max's girl) & she is very pleased with them. She has just asked me to make her wedding dress but I am afraid I will have to refuse as I have not much time.

Well, I think I have written enough of myself. As soon as you receive this letter please answer & let me know if I am forgiven & how you are getting on. We all here are keeping well. I hope this letter finds you the same.

It may interest you to know that Doris Ramm (the girl

Max was engaged to when you were here) is now married, they all say here that she lost now [no] time, in a way we are glad & so is Max.

I will now close hoping to hear from you soon, with my best love & kisses to you.

Yours very Sincerely,
Eva

P.S. Please give my regards to your father & sister.

83 Chatham St.
Liverpool 7
30/3/38

Dear Morris,

I was very delighted to receive your very welcome letter to-day. Although I do not yet know if you have forgiven me, the letter shows at least that you are not angry with me. I am patiently waiting for an answer to my last weeks letter that everything is alright between us again & that it will not be long now before we are both together.

I have told my family that I am sorry now that I did not marry you when you were here. They are sorry too for having stood in the way but I know deep down that I would not have been happy had I known that my family were against us. It was only the thought of missing me that made them do it. Mother specially is upset & is hoping that everything will be alright & the sight of your letter this morning brightened her up.

I have suffered too the last few weeks but through my own fault. I realise now that you are the only boy for me & I could never care for anyone else.

I wanted to correct the wrong accusation you made of Beatie Socolove but I felt I had no right to be angry with you after the way I had treated you & you could not help it. I only saw Beatie for a short time[.] [S]he did not mention your name to me. You hurt me very much by saying that you sup-

Beattie Sokolov.

posed I had become fickled & petted by some one else[.] [Y]ou know that I am not that kind of girl even when I went with Isador Alper, which thank goodness was only a very short time, I never let him make love to me, & you also hurt me by saying that I had been playing with you all the time. The words I gave you when you were here last March that I was not playing with you were sincerely true.

You ask me what I bought with the 5 dollars you sent for my birthday, strange as it may seem I have never spent it. I do not know why but I have not wanted to change it to English money, but if all is well between us I will buy something for my trousseau with it.

You should not have refused the invitations from Norman [Jackson], after all you have to go out & enjoy yourself. I hope very soon to be going with you on your visits to Auntie Jean & Norman & to make up for the invitations you turned down.

In the middle of writing this letter Leah called with her sister, the one who broke her arm when you were here. I am making a two piece for her. Leah asked me about you & I told her that I had made a mess of things, she laughingly told me that true love never runs smooth. She sends her kindest regards to you.

We are all very excited over Max's wedding. When I have finished this letter I will have to start cutting out our dresses as time is getting shorter & I have only the evenings in which to do them.

All through this winter I have been going to Keep-fit

classes at our deaf club, last week we gave a Health & Grace Demonstration at Bootle & it went off very well.

We all here are keeping well[.] [H]oping this letter finds you the same.

I will now close,
With best love & kisses to you

Your's
Eva

P.S. Kindest regards from my parents & family.

83 Chatham St.
Liverpool 7
13/4/38

Dear Morris,

    I was very pleased to receive your welcome letter. I had expected you to be angry with me but I never expected such a bitter letter from you. Many girls have done much worse than I did & have been forgiven. You say that by the way I acted I have crushed the love you had for me. I am wondering now, if your love had ever been deep[.] [I]f it had you would not have been so bitter to-wards me. I did not balance your love with Isadore Alpers, as I have never felt any to-ward him, ours had been only pure friendship nothing more.

    You say that I have never said that I love you in any of the letters that I have written to you, have I not told you before that I am no good in expressing my love for you in black & white. But I will say this that I love you very deeply & always have & I have realized the last few weeks that I love you even deeper. Every time after I had written angry letters to you I have always apologised right away, do you think I would do this if I did not love you. [E]ven when I was with Isadore I always thought about you & wished it was you instead of him. I am not blaming you for being angry with me but why such bitterness. Do you remember when you stopped writing to me the summer when you were in London. I heard some gossip that you were going about with the younger girls. Yet when you started again with me after we met at Warrington I did not mention this to you when you said that you had been too busy to write to me all the time.*

You also write that you will be fair to me & will marry me, although you do not love me as much as before. Morris you would be doing me a great wrong if you do, only if you love me will I marry you, if you still find the bitterness for me in your heart instead of the love you once had we could never be happy, in spite of everything I still love you, Morris.

You say that my treatment of you has automatically realised [released] you from your promises about going back to England for good. I don't & never did expect you to give up a good job[.] [I]f ever I am your wife I would stay where ever you wanted me to, in America for good if you say so.

My parents & family think very highly of you & always have, try & understand that it is only the parting that made them do what they did.

I am going to write to Janie now & will explain everything about the Consulate to her.

Kindest regards from my family & best love & kisses to you.

Yours
Eva

---

* Eva must be referring to letters that precede the ones in this collection. Morris refers in his letter to the fact that they met each for "one hour" at the Warrington Deaf Club. Then he was supposed to follow up this visit, but had to cancel his trip. Apparently Eva and Morris's mutual friend Beattie Sokolov may have had something to do with introducing them. *Ed.*

32 Meserole St.,
Brooklyn, New York
U.S. America
April 24th, 1938

My dear Eva,

I was very glad to receive your letter last Friday morning, and as it was Yomtov [the holiday], and I do not write letters on Yomtov and Sabbath, I had to wait patiently till today, Sunday, when I have the extreme pleasure of writing to you again. I know you had already got my last two letters last Thursday or Friday, and I hope you were made happy by these two letters which told you of my happiness and love for you better than my first letter which made you feel upset. I did feel upset too, when I read your letter, and I am very sorry about my letter making you feel upset. However, I was being frank and of course you don't want me to pretend and be hypocritic, and you cannot blame me for being embittered. Eva, I assure you I was not bitter toward you, but I was angry with you for keeping secret your affair with Isadore Alper from me since last December, and also when you sent me the letter last February about your not wanting to come to America, you still did not give me any explanation. I was not mad at you for going to Isadore and giving me the air, because it was your own business, even if he tried to steal you by underhand and mean tricks. Only it was *quite wrong* of you not to let me know right away the change of your heart. I also thought to myself

Morris's girlfriend?

that you should stick to Isadore instead of coming back to me, because I did not like to be second fiddle to any other boy. Please believe me, I have never felt bitter toward you, but only bitterness about our misunderstanding in general. You say that you were wondering if my love had ever been deep. Perhaps you will wonder differently if I tell you how much I suffered for almost ten weeks and how I lost 9 lbs. in weight within a few weeks, although I neglected my training in my [track and field] club. When I sent you my last two letters, I had not an iota of bitterness in my heart at all and I had forgiven you completely and wholeheartedly for the way you treated me. Please dear Eva, let us forget everything about the past misunderstanding and write no more about it. I was surprised you cared when I stopped writing to you the Summer when I was in London after we had seen each other at your club in Liverpool for only one short hour or so. If I had known you cared, I would have continued writing to you in spite of my wounded pride, which Beattie Sockolov caused me for cancelling my visit to Manchester because of having to see my sister, Janie off on her visit to America and Beattie calling me far too slow and suggesting that I try to have you. You remember me telling you all this at Warrington, so you must have been mistaken about my telling you that I was too busy to write to you all the time, because I don't remember telling you about being too busy to write to you. After stopping to write to you and Beattie, because of my foolish pride, I began to go about with other girls because of myself being fancy-free, although I thought of you both very often. I would never play you false. Only yesterday at the deaf club affair, I told one of the girl friends about you, when she grew persistent about my taking her out, although she knew I did not care for her and other girl friends. Last month in trying to forget my sorrow and trouble about you, I took her out *only once*, I gave her a good time, although I failed to forget you and enjoy myself. When she asked me about you last month, I only said that it was very hard for you to come to America. Since then I have been trying to keep away from the girl friends. Now dear Eva, we will look forward to being together again very soon, and write nice letters to each other about our hopes, future, your love, my love; about your dresses, your family and deaf friends etc. Now come to think of it, you can start preparing your trousseau now, because if you are told to marry me on the ship before landing in New York, we want to have a regular wedding ceremony and there are synagogues and Kosher tables for Jewish passengers in the big liners. Auntie Jean said that if we have to be married on the boat, she would take care of everything about getting a rabbi and other necessary things. Of course you, dear Eva, and I want you to wear a wedding dress and veil, so please try to get them and bring them with you, when you come to America, Please God. If you fail to get the permanent visa from the Consulate in London, please apply for the visitor's visa either in Liverpool or London and in this case, it will not be necessary for you to mention about me at all. Just say you are visiting Uncle and Auntie Winarick and other three Aunts for six months. Then after a short time when we get married, we go to Canada for a few weeks' honeymoon, and then we can apply to the Consulate General in Canada and apply for your permanent visa to come back to America with me because of your status as a wife of an American Citizen. All these are lawful and legal and cheaper and more convenient than my going to England to marry you. I hope you will let me know as soon as you hear from the Consulate in London and all about your visit to London for Max' wedding. My love to your family. Annie said she was happy about everything between you and me, and give you a big hug and love. She said she sent you her pictures and would like to know what you think of them and write to her. My Best Love and Kisses xxx to you.

Yours,
Morris

83, Chatham St.
Liverpool 7,
24/4/38

Dear Morris,

    I received your very welcome letter on Thursday & as it was Yomtov I could not answer your letter right away. I also received your letter of April 13th. I was glad to read in your letters that you do not feel anymore bitterness towards me now. After reading your last letter I can understand that you did not really mean what you wrote in your letter of April 4th that you do not love me anymore. I sincerely hope that everything will be alright between us now & that it will not be long before we are together again for always.

    I am enclosing the reply I got from the American Consulate. I am also enclosing the forms I received on November 3rd. I told you last November that I had received the forms from the Consulate but as he only asked for affidavits, I did not think it was much good sending them as I had only a month before showed him the affidavits from my Aunties. I have still got the other affidavits. Please tell me in your next letter if I should send them to the Consulate. I do not understand quite clearly what I have to do. I think it would be better if you send the necessary papers direct to the Consulate as it will save time & trouble. I received a card from Janie saying that she will go to the Consulate General tomorrow. She may be able to impress him that you are sincere in your wish to marry me. She wrote that she was too busy last week to go. Janie thought I was in America & was surprised to get my letter. Whatever made her think so? I would have liked to invite Janie & your mother to Max's wedding but Ann's father asked Max not to invite too many people as he does not want to make a very big wedding, so I left it all to Max. I will try & slip round to see Janie if I have any time. How did you enjoy the Passover holidays. I kept thinking of last year when you were here dear Morris & I hope that next year we will [be] celebrating our first Passover together. You ask me if I still wish to marry you now that your earnings are less than before. I have told you before that your money means nothing to me & I still wish to marry you. I will have to learn to budget expenses as you say. Norman's wife does. Now don't laugh at me. Give my kindest regards to Norman & his wife when you see them next.

How are you keeping & also your father & sister. I am pleased to say that we all here are well.

With best love & kisses to you,

Yours
Eva

P.S. Kindest regards from the family

In Reply Refer to
File No. 811.11 - MAC: evh

The Foreign Service
of the
United States of America

American Consulate General
1 Grosvenor Square
London, W.1.
April 22, 1938

Miss Eva Weintrope [sic]
83 Chatham Street,
Liverpool 7

Madam:

In reply to your letter of April 20th, I beg to inform
you that it was suggested in a communication from this office
dated November 3, 1937, that affidavits of support from your
aunts in the United States would be necessary before proceed-
ing with your visa application.

The Consulate General has received an affidavit from
your uncle, Mr. Arthur Winarick. However, Mr. Winarick
has failed to prove his alleged income and savings and until
such evidence is received it is not believed advisable for you to
come to London. Should you receive any additional evidence
concerning your uncle's earnings and savings or affidavits of

support from your aunts together with proof of their incomes and savings and forward it here the Consulate General will be pleased to examine it.

> Very truly yours,
> Douglas Jenkins
> American Consul General

[This letter was enclosed by Eva with the previous letter.]

"Dear Eva of My Own"

May 3, 1938 to August 25, 1938

Max (Eva's brother) and Ann at their wedding.

83 Chatham St.
Liverpool 7
3/5/37[38]

Dear Morris,

I was very pleased to receive your welcome letter this morning. It made me very happy now that I know that everything is alright & I agree with you that we should forget the past & misunderstanding & not write anymore about it.

Max's wedding was a lovely affair & we all enjoyed ourselves very much. I kept thinking about you all the time & wished you were with me. Ann's people are very nice & friendly[.] [I]t was the first time the family's had met except the parents. There were about 23 from Liverpool & we had a Saloon compartment reserved. We had to leave at 11.30 pm to catch the train & this morning we had a card from Max to say that it was a pity we had to leave early as they danced until 2 A.M. Joe & his wife stayed on overnight.

Janie['s] place was just the next street so I slipped around at six but there was no one in & a note to say they would be back at 8 o'clock. I went round again at nine. Janie was very pleased to see me & wanted me to stay longer. She said that she had been to the Consulate & he told her that Uncle Arther [Arthur] should send a letter from his banker stating how much money he has and also from someone who has known Uncle a long time, about his business, that he is the boss, & how he is doing. Tell Uncle Arther to send the necessary papers direct to the Consulate. I will also write to Uncle.

Janie thinks that everything will be alright if Uncle furnishes the papers & I hope, Morris dear, that it will not now be long before we are to-gether again.

Of course I want to wear a white wedding dress & veil when I get married, my family would not like it otherwise. I don't think we will have to get married on the ship as Uncle & Auntie are claiming me, in this case I would prefer to have my wedding dress made in America as I would want to have the very latest style. If I fail with the permanent visa I will do as you say & apply for a visitors visa, but Morris I am wondering would they suspect something if I had previously applied for a permanent visa & was refused. Anyway I hope it will not be necessary for me to apply for the visitors visa. Yes I received Annie's letter & photo's. I had wanted to write to her before but was waiting for things to clear up between us before writing to her & will do so soon.

Ester Graft & her husband (excuse me for not putting her married name) called at Queen's Hill to take me round to the Deaf Club, but I did not go as I wanted to see Janie & time was getting short. Annie Rubin wrote & told them about the wedding. Ray & her husband Abraham Lazarus & the baby also came round to see me. Ray was my old school friend. They asked me when I was getting married, so I told them about you.

My brother Joe asked me about you[.] [H]e knew there was something the matter & asked me if things were alright now. In the middle of the dinner at the wedding a telegram came from Elkan (Joe's little boy) wishing Max & Ann

Mazletov ["good luck" in Yiddish]. They did not want to drag Elkan all the way for a day so left him with friends in Swansea.

Max will live in Tredegar South Wales, we already miss him & it is very quite [quiet] at home without any boys & Max was always the "life of the party."

I have some private work for customers of my own. I had been putting off doing them to make the wedding dresses, so as soon as, I have finished them I will start making my own trousseau. P.G. [Please God].

All bad workers blame their tools[.] Well I am blaming my pen for the terrible writing.

With kindest regards from my family & my very best love & kisses xxxx to you.

Your's Own
Eva

Kindest regard to your father & sister

83 Chatham St.
Liverpool 7
19/5/38

Dear Morris,

Many thanks for your very nice letter. I had been expecting it since last week & only received it yesterday. I noticed the post mark was the 5th. It had taken nearly two weeks to reach me. Anyway I was very glad to receive your letter & read its contents. I must say your letters are very interesting to read. I don't think mine are half as much. Yes, it is nice to receive our letters at the same time & answer each others at the same time.

Yes, I knew that Celia Harrison [Eva's cousin, daughter of her aunt Mollie Harrison née Chmielewski] is stenographer at Uncle Arthurs place as Max told us when he was in America. I believe her father works there in a small way.

I should also be surprised if your letter does not impress the Consul General. I hope he will take a kinder attitude. If not we have Uncles papers. The consul only kept your affidavit of support & returned the other papers to me. In my letter to the consulate last month I told him about your intentions of wanting to come to England last Nov. 17th & of my sending you the cablegram telling you to cancel your passage. So you can see, it is alright that we have both said the same thing. I am waiting for a letter from the Consulate telling me to go to London for the visa & please God, if I get one I will promise you that I will not keep you waiting long before I sail

to America. I would like to spend a few days or so in Swansea
with Joe & Rosy [Eva's brother and sister-in-law], as I had
not seen them for over a year, when I saw them for a few hours
at Max's wedding. We had a letter from Auntie Jean & she
writes that she is very pleased that everything is alright between us. She said that I should not have mentioned to you
about the Leeds boy & so did father, but I told him that it is
always best to tell the truth, than you should find out later on
from someone else. It sounds nice, apartment rooms, three
rooms & and bathroom, just what I would like. I will leave it
to you in which part of America as you know best[.] [A]ny-
thing that suits you will do for me.

   I am very glad & happy Morris & I do love you very
much. I am waiting for the day when you will be telling me
that there is too much pepper & not enough salt.

   I had a letter from Janie. She writes that she was waiting for me the morning after the wedding [Max's wedding].
I was surprised as I had told her I had only come down on
an excursion.

   She writes that I should write & ask Uncle [Arthur
Winarick] to send a letter from his banker & also a letter from
some authority stating their weekly or monthly earnings or
taking, she also writes that Uncle should send proof of his willingness & ability to keep me until my marriage.

   I would like an engagement ring but if you do not want
to bother with one, we will not argue about it. The ring once
bought is for a lifetime.

   The King and Queen are paying Liverpool the honour
of a visit to-day. They are I believe already here[.] [W]e have

been given an hour & half off from work to see the Royal visitors. I am taking advantage of the time off by writing this letter to you. They are making a four day's tour of Lancashire. We will have to work late to-night, as we are very busy and have been these last few weeks.

A friend of Betty's [Eva's sister] told her that I am having so much bother in getting a visa I should go to Canada & get married there. Then I would get a permanent visa there, if for any reason I fail to get the visa here. We will see about my going to Canada, as it would be much easier.

As I have to be back at 1 o'clock & it is nearly that now I will have to close now.

With all my love to you dear Morris,

Your's own,
Eva

83 Chatham St.
Liverpool 7
May 19th 38

Dear Morris,

You will no doubt be surprised to hear from me but I would just like to wish you and Eva the very best of luck together.

I am very glad that all the misunderstanding between you both have been smoothed out, mother & father are also very pleased that everything is now perfect between you both. I would like you to understand that at first we made it hard for Eva to decide definitely about going to America, as we did not want such a lovely girl (which you already know perfectly well) to leave us, anyhow we hope now that it will not be long before Eva is able to join you, we are all quite excited about it at home, in fact I just feel as though I would love to make the trip myself.

I hope you are keeping well.

Mother, father and all send our fondest wishes.

> Your future sister-in-law
> Betty

[This letter was enclosed with the previous one.]

Betty (Eva's sister).

83 Chatham St.
Liverpool 7
26/5/38

Dear Morris,

Many thanks for your very welcome letter. It was nice to come home after a hard day's work & find your letter. I enjoyed reading it over my supper.

I have been waiting patiently for a letter from the Consulate in answer to the letter you sent him but have not yet received one. I suppose they are waiting for Uncle Arthurs papers. I hope you have by the time you get this letter already have sent them on.

It is considered unlucky for a bride to made [make] her own wedding dress. I would not make it myself either here or in America, even Celia did not make her own wedding dress but had it made by another dressmaker. If we do have to get married on the boat don't you think it would look ridiculous for me to change into a white wedding dress and veil only for the ceremony & then change soon after. I have always wanted to be married in white, but never thought it may have to be on a boat, would any of our relations be able to witness the ceremony. Let us hope we will be allowed to wait a little while & have a proper wedding in America.

Max has just sent us the wedding photos. Separate ones for Betty & myself saying we would eventually have our own homes, very thoughtful of him isn't it. They are lovely photos, Max looks very handsome in his tails & Ann too looks lovely. The family keep telling me that they are waiting until I send them our wedding photos. Our sewing machine is too old fashioned to take to America[.] [W]e have had it nearly twenty years. I had been thinking for some time of getting an electric cabinet machine, but it would not be worth while now. I could get one in America. I am keeping well hoping this letter finds you the same. With very best wishes from the family and my very best love and kisses to you.

    Yours ever
    Eva

32 Meserole St,
Brooklyn, New York
U.S. America
May 27th 1938

Dear Eva,

I was very pleased to receive your most welcome letter
this morning. I was very surprised to find a strange handwritten letter inside when I opened your letter, so I looked at the
end of the letter for the name. I guess I was not patient enough
to read the letter first instead of looking for the name first, but
I could not help it. I was very pleased to hear from Betty and it
was very nice of her and I thank her very much for her good
wishes.

I am sincerely very pleased to know that I am in good
graces of your whole family now, because I do really love your
family, and it was in your house, dear Eva, I spent my most
pleasant times of my life, when I was in England last year. I am
sorry you waited rather long for the letter, but I could not help
it, because I found at the post-office that there were no fast liners sailing for England at that time. I always look at the list of
foreign mailing and names of mail steamships on the walls of
all post offices and also in the newspapers with Shipping
pages. That is why I always write the names of the fastest liners on the envelopes of the letters I send you so that the letters
may catch these boats just in time before they sail, and I also
know what ships with mails from England are expected to

_1_

32 Meserole St.,
Brooklyn, New York,
U. S. America.
May 27ᵈ. 1938.

Dear Eva,

I was very pleased to receive your most welcome letter this morning. I was very surprised to find a strange handwritten letter inside when I opened your letter, so I looked at the end of the letter for the name. I guess I was not patient enough to read the letter first instead of looking for the name first, but I could not help it. I was very pleased to hear from Betty and it was very nice of her and I thank her very much for her good wishes.

An excerpt of a letter from Morris to Eva, May 27, 1938.

arrive in New York and in that way I expected your letter this morning. I am answering your letter right away, as there are no fast liners sailing till next Wednesday, and I hope you will receive it on June 6th or 7th.

Last Wednesday morning, as there were no work in my shop that morning, I took an opportunity of going to Uncle Arthur's factory to find out the reason of getting any news about the papers from Washington as his secretary, Mr. Patsiner promised to let me know within a short time. Uncle Arthur was not there, but Mr. Patsiner said that Auntie Jean had the letters from their bank and they would not wait for the photostat of income tax receipts from Washington as it would be several months before they get these papers from Washington. Mr. Patsiner promised to mail the letters from the Bank direct to the Consul General next week, when Uncle and Aunt Winarick return from the country, where they are now[,] next Wednesday. He gave me a pleasant surprise package and then I hurried back to work and then when I got home in the evening, I opened the package eagerly and here I found several large bottles of hair tonic, and shampoo, after shaving lotion, hair bristle brush, talcum powder, etc. Father looked interested and looked in the package like Christmas stocking to see if there were any more. I was thinking of you, Eva dear, as I opened the package and packed it up again and put it in the clothes closet (cupboard) till the day you come to America, Please God, and show it to you.

You did absolutely quite right about telling me about the other boy, because if you had not done so while wanting me to take you back, I would not have given you a hundred per cent love if mixed with suspicions, wondering, incredulities, disbelieves, etc. As it is, I love you very much with no trace of bitterness, distrust, and coldness, because I know you had a try with a different boy and you realized that you could not love any other boy and that you love me much more and want me more than ever, and now I know I can safely trust you and you are now more sincere than before you went out with the other boy. Please, dear Eva, let us forget all about what happened as far as the other boy is concerned. You and I want to write about ourselves.

I am enclosing the money order for £ 20 for the engagement ring for you, Darling Eva; and I wish you the very Best of Happiness in wearing your engagement ring and I hope you will enjoy a long and healthy life in wearing the engagement ring. I am also sending one dollar extra for the expenses to pay to the registered and genuine assayer in a different shop to examine the genuineness of the ring before paying for the ring. Please have someone who is experienced in the jewelry to accompany you. I believe Jack Ross [Eva's brother-in-law] knows something about it. Now, dear Eva, are you happy? I hope so.

My kindest regards to your family and my best love and kisses xxxxx to you, dear Eva darling.

I am Yours Very Sincerely,
Morris

P.S. Dear Eva, I am here in a Post Office, and I have just issued the money order form naming Jack Ross as the reciepant [recipient] of the money (£ 20-4-0) to cash the two money orders in Liverpool, 7 Post Office. I gave your address on the form, as I don't know Jack's new address with his father. Please tell your father to let my mother know about our engagement and your engagement ring as soon as you have the ring, as it is usual for the girl's parents to announce her engagement. I hope you will be wearing the ring when you write your next letter to me. Did the Consul send you back my letter from Washington, I sent you last April 4th? If so, please save it, as it will prove useful when you land in America. Love xxxxx Morris

83 Chatham St.
Liverpool 7
3/6/38

My Dearest Morris,

I have only just come home from work & imagine my surprise to find your letter waiting for me. Darling I don't know how to thank you for sending me the 100 dollars for the ring. I hope that when I put it on it will be the beginning of every happiness for us both. I only wish you were near enough to put it on for me and I hope that I will be able to make you very happy as I know you deserve to be. I will buy the ring off a reliable person. He is a friend of the family & Max also bought his ring from this fellow. I will have the ring tested before I purchase it.

I have not yet heard from the Consulate. A friend of our's was here last night, she also has lived in America for a number of years & wants to go back again. I told her about the trouble I am having with the Consulate. She was very good & told me that if I do not hear soon from London, I should go to her sister who lives in Canada, & we could get married there then go back to America. What do you say to this Morris! I think it would be a very good idea if I am refused a visa the second time or if I have to wait too long. It would not be fair to Auntie Jean if I went on a Visitor's Visa as she will have to put up a lot of money then probably lose it all. I am answering this letter right away as it is Friday & if I do not write now I will not be able to write until Tuesday as it is Yomtov. Mother is starting to light the candles, so I will have to close. I thank you once more, Dear Morris & wish you a very pleasant & happy Yomtov.

My family are also very pleased about the ring & send you their very best regards.

With best love & kisses to you Dear xxx

Your Own,
Eva

32 Meserole St.,
Brooklyn, New York,
U.S. America
June 6th, 1938

My dear Eva,

I was very glad to receive your most welcome letter last
Friday at the same time as a letter from Mr. Patsiner, Uncle
Arthur's secretary telling me that he had already sent two
letters from the two banks and another letter from Uncle
Arthur's corporation (firm) directly to the Consul General the
previous day. I had already told Mr. Patsiner and Aunt Jean
that I had rather not sent them to the Consul myself because I
did not want to pry into Uncle Winarick's personal affairs.
You will be surprised the same as Father, Uncle and Aunt
Winarick and I felt, because I received a very long and nice personal letter from the Consul General, Mr. Douglas Jenkins,
himself last Saturday, the day after I received your letter. I did
not expect him to answer my long letter of May 4th, but I
hoped he would write to you. My letter certainly impressed
him as I told you that I hoped, because he sent me the letter
very long equal to eight pages of my letter to him. He explained everything in details from your appointment with
him last October 12th to now. He waited one week in vain for
the papers from Uncle Arthur as I promised him and so he
sent me that long letter, asking me about the papers from
Uncle Arthur. He said that he would have granted you the visa

last October 12th if you had answered him that you were willing to marry immediately on arriving in America. Since you said you did not want to get married immediately and that you wanted to wait a few weeks in New York so as to prepare for the religious wedding, he said he had no power to grant you the visa as under the law. I wish you had answered him that you were willing to get married immediately on arrival in America, because you and I would have been spared misunderstandings and so much sufferings. Father said we could have [planned to have] the religious wedding in a few days or weeks again in New York after our marriage on the boat the same as many Jewish people did. Now what had been done could not be helped, so we will have to look forward to our future. The Consul wrote that you will be sure to get your visa as soon as he gets the necessary papers from Uncle Winarick, P.G. [Please God] Today is exactly one year since I returned to America, and it was a very long wait for me. I am glad you said you would not keep me waiting long before you sail, because you will feel it worth suffering so much when you come to America this month. If you receive a letter with an appointment from the Consul, you can spend a few days with Joe and Rosie before or after going to London, and please give my best regards to them. Please . . . [missing]

P.S. Aunt Jean showed me the letter with postcard photo of wedding from Max, who wrote about your willingness to travel to America & he also hopes to go to America with Ann for a visit in about 2 years.

32 Meserole St.,
Brooklyn, New York,
U.S. America.
June 16th 1938

Dear Eva,

I was very glad to receive your most welcome letter yesterday and I was also very pleased to know that you were very happy to get the engagement ring. Now dear Eva we are actually engaged, isn't it nice? It is also very nice you called me Darling for the first time and I sure like it, and you can see now how easy it is for you to express your feeling in your letters, whenever you feel like doing so. Since we started together again last April, we have been sending each other nice and smoothly written letters with no more uncertainties, and we are more than ever very good friends and I hope for always. Father, Annie [Morris's sister] and Aby, my brother, are also very pleased about the engagement ring, and I am waiting to hear from Mother and Janie whether they learned about the ring from your family. You say you hope you will be able to make me very happy as I deserve to be, yes, you will make me very happy by coming to me very, very soon. I hope by now you have already heard from the Consulate. I don't think we will have to worry about whether you will get the visa or not.

However if anything unforeseen arise[s] and you are refused the visa again, I think it will be best for you to go to Montreal, Canada within two weeks as Uncle Winarick advised and Father agreed that it is best what Uncle Winarick thinks. You will have to agree to marry immediately upon arrival in Canada, but we shall also have a religious wedding in New York after we leave Canada. All these are what Uncle and Auntie Winarick suggested. In that case please remember to ask the consul in London to return *all* the affidavits and papers of Uncle Arthur's and mine to you if he again refuses to give you the visa, because the papers of Uncle Winarick's will come very handy when you appear before the Canadian Immigration Authorities in Montreal. Don't show them the affidavits of support, but keep them to show to the American Consul in Canada when we go there for your visa. Anyway I hope you will get the visa from the Consul General in London to come to America, but if you are again refused the visa, please don't write to me asking me to tell you what to do, but go to the Cunard White Star Line at once and book a passage to Montreal, Canada and then let Auntie Jean and me know the name of the boat and the date of sailing, so that we may be there to meet you, dearest, when you get off the boat. I hope to have you with me very soon, my own girl. Best regards to your family, and I close with my best love and kisses xxx to you, my own engaged girl friend—sweetheart Eva xxx

Yours always,
Morris

In Reply Refer to
File No. 811.11 - ESM/fh

The Foreign Service
of the
United States of America

American Consulate General
London, England, June 17, 1938

Mr. Morris Davis
32 Meserole Street,
Brooklyn, New York

Sir:

The receipt is acknowledged of your letter of June 6, 1938 referring further to the visa application of your fiancée, Miss Eva Weintrobe.

I have the pleasure in informing you that the Consulate General is now in receipt of evidence which would appear to establish that Miss Weintrobe is not likely to become a public charge if admitted to the United States for permanent residence. She is being given an appointment for July 6 to appear at this office for a reconsideration of her visa application.

Very truly yours,
Douglas Jenkins,
American Consul General

83 Chatham St.
Liverpool 7
15/6/38

My dear Morris,

I was very glad to receive your very welcome letter yesterday. I also received a letter yesterday from the Consulate General for my appointment on July 6th[,] from your letter I now feel sure of getting the visa this time & I hope P.G. to sail about the 23rd or 30th of next month. I am anxiously waiting for the day when we will be together again for always. I was very interested in what you wrote of the Consul, but I was surprised that he was not speaking the truth when he said that I wanted to wait a few weeks after my arrival in America for a religious wedding. Betty too was very surprised as she remembers my telling the Consul that I was prepared to marry you very soon after my arrival in America or on the boat if necessary. [N]othing at all was suggest[ed] about a religious wedding then. [I]t was after when we tried the second time to get the visa that we both suggest[ed] about the religious wedding as the reason of my sending you the cablegram. I had not heard from Janie for some time so I wrote to her yesterday & told her of my appointment.

I have got a lovely engagement ring, it is a single stone in platinum with diamond shoulders. Everytime I put it on I feel very proud of it. You were a dear to send me the money. The girls at work & the [Deaf] Club look at it with envy. I

always feel nearer to you when I have it on. Father has been
down to change the money order, but they say that it has not
yet come through & would probably by the end of this week.
The fellow we got the ring off was down last night for the
money, he said he would try & change it through his bank,
so father gave him the money order. The ring was valued at
£22.10 but afterwards he dropped it to £20. I am making myself a brown costume I will need it for travelling to London, &
am starting to get the rest of my cloths together. I am going to
ask Celia to make my wedding dress as I think you are right
about taking a wedding dress & viel [veil] with me.

I have told the crowd at the Club & workshop that I
will be leaving soon. They all keep telling me how much they
will miss me & when they will be loosing [losing] me. The mis-
sioner at our Club, you remember seeing him at Warrington
was very pleased to hear of our engagement & sends you his
very best wishes. Annie & Ada Rubin & Leah Purcell also
send their very best wishes. It was nice of Auntie Jean to take
so much interest. I will write to her when I get my visa & let
her know when I am ready to sail.

Mother has gone to Swansea for her annual holiday.
She has not been too well lately so I hope the holiday will do
her good. Max & Ann may probably come here next week as
Max['s] pal is getting married[.] [W]e are all invited Betty & I
may go too.

I received a letter this morning from Ray Lazarus. She
heard about my engagement & sent good wishes, it is really

wonderful how fast news travels. I will try & see her when I am in London.

Harold, bless him asked me if he can be page boy at my wedding. I told him I would love him too, but none of the family were coming to my wedding. He said not even Baba [Grandma] Weintrobe[.] He is making good progress at school & is getting quite a big lad. He keeps telling me that he does not want me to go away, first it was Max & now me. He seems to be very fond of our family.

Please give my kindest regards to your father & sister, did she receive the letter I sent her. With best love & kisses xxxx to you.

Eva

83 Chatham St.
Liverpool 7
28/6/38

Dear Morris,

I was very pleased to receive your ever welcome letter.
I received your letter the same time as one from Janie. I wrote
to her telling of my appointment at the Consulate on July 6th
& had not heard from her so I wrote again. She was very surprised to get my second letter as she had already written &
told me that she would be pleased to come with me to the Consulate. I never received the letter[.] [I]t must have got mislaid
in the post. Joe wrote that he would be in London this week &
asked me if I would like him to pay Janie a visit. I told him to
go as I had then not heard from Janie. It does not seem necessary now, still they can both have a chat. I am thinking of
going to London the evening before my appointment as you
know how I hate travelling overnight. I suppose Janie will
be able to put me up for one night.

I am glad you are happy too over our engagement.
I am waiting for the day when I will be able to show you
the ring. I find it easy now to express my feelings in writing,
whereas I was too shy before. I am glad you like it. I hope
from now on we will both never have any more uncertainties
& misunderstanding.

I had to have my passport renewed as it expired on 5th
April. On asking at the Office why I had been given only six

months I was told that if a person goes over to get married they are given the passport for a short time. I have got all my other papers together.

I will leave work the Friday after I get my visa as I want to be ready to sail as soon as I can. I shall have a far[e]well party before a [I] leave work & also a small one at home for my close friends. I will write to you after my visit to the Consulate. I am waiting for the day, dear, when I will see you once again for always.

With best Love & kisses xxx to you

Your's own
Eva

83 Chatham St.
Liverpool 7
7/7/38

Dear Morris,

I am now home & very happy & excited as I have got
my visa & know you will be happy too when you read this letter & know that everything has turned out as we wanted it to
be. I went to London on Tuesday afternoon & as no one was
at the Station to meet me I went straight to Janie's place. She
made me very welcome during my stay with her. Janie & a
friend of hers came with me to the Consulate, but she was not
allowed to come inside with me. She had to wait in an outer
office. I went through it all alone but was not a bit nervous.
After being examined by a doctor I was taken into the Consulate's Office, at first I thought it was Mr. Jenkins, but he signed
his name on my papers as Mr. Colebrook[.] [T]owards the
end of my interview with him another man came in[.] I
guessed it was Mr. Jenkins although I was not told his name,
he smiled to me & jokingly asked if I was not already married.
After I had my visa & was on my way out I met him again & I
thanked him personally. I went back to Janie's & had some
tea. Then I went to Ray Lazarus['] place to say good-by. She
was out but her husband was in & he took me to her mother's
where I found her. She was very pleased to see me & begged
me to stay another night at her house. I had intended going
back by the 8.45 P.M. train, but I stayed another day. Ray

came with me to visit some friends of our family in Stoke New-
ington. They were also very pleased to see me & were very
glad to hear the good news of my getting the visa. I stayed
with them the last time I was refused the visa. They asked me
at the Consulate who was paying my fare over[.] I did not like
to say that I was as they may think it funny so I replied that
you had already sent the money over. If they ask you on the
other side, don't forget to say that you paid as I do not want
things to get mixed up. Of course I do not mind paying the
fare but it is best if the others do not know. I had intended going tourists (second class) but I was told it would be better if
I go third class as I will not be so lonesome & that they are
quite nice people travelling third. Now Morris please be reasonable[.] [I]t is quite impossible for me to sail on the 16th of
this month, although I want to do anything to please you &
never want to disappoint you. I would never manage to get
things together in time. Please do not be vexed with me. I will
book my passage for July 30th as it is impossible for me to sail
before. You say you will not be very happy if I do not sail on
the 16th that you will always have a trace of sadness. Morris
are you going to let two weeks of waiting spoil our whole life
of happiness[?]

    [H]ad I got my visa earlier I would have been able to
sail sooner. Please Morris do not be vexed with me[.] [T]he
time will soon fly. I told Janie that you wanted me to sail on
the 16th, she also said that it would be too much of a rush and
it would be better for me to go at the end of this month. I think
we will have to married on the boat as the Consulate asked me

if I would be prepared to marry you on arrival in America. I replied that I would. I will write to Auntie Jean as soon as I book my passage as I would like her to be at the boat to meet me also. I dread the parting with my family and I know it will be very hard for us all especially mother. I hope P.G. I will never regret the day that I had taken these steps, that we will both never do anything to hurt the other, that we will always be happy in each others company. I received your letter the morning that I went to London. Celia went to Swansea yesterday for a two weeks stay[.] [B]oth she & Harold have not been too well, when she comes back she will make my Wedding Dress. I went round to my workshop this afternoon & told them that I am leaving to-morrow. They are all sorry I am going also the boss. They have asked me what I would like for a Wedding present. I am having a small farewell party there to-morrow night.

I will close now, my family sends you their very best regards. I also send my regards to your father sister & brother. Your mother came round to see me yesterday morning, she looked quite well. With all my love to you & kisses xxx

Your's ever
Eva

32 Meserole St.,
Brooklyn, New York,
U.S.A.
July 19th 1938

My dearest Eva,

I was very glad to receive your nice letter yesterday, and I waited till lunch hour now to answer your letter, as I thought I would get another letter from you this morning, but my father brought a letter from Janie to me in my shop, when I went down for lunch today. My boss kindly let me write this letter in his office. I have only half an hour to spare before starting to work again this afternoon. Perhaps you forgot to tell me the name of boat you are sailing on July 30th. I am rushing this letter so that "Queen Mary" may bring it to you next Tuesday just before you sail, and I hope you will have time to write a few lines to me again before your sail. I was surprised yesterday when I learned that my brother Aby is getting married on August 20th, and I, being older than him, hope you and I will be able to get married after all before my birthday [August 26]. Janie wrote that if we get married on the boat, it will be only a civil ceremony, and then on about August 14th we will have a religious wedding, which I always had wanted to have here. Annie will help me look for our new home before you arrive and then when you arrive, you and I will choose over our own style furnitures, etc. I am going to write to Auntie Jean tomorrow and ask for her to arrange for our wedding with Annie to help me as my mother's representative. I am excited at the prospect of seeing you again very soon after such a long time, dear Eva. I hope you will enjoy yourself very much during your trip on the high seas, and please take good care of yourself and enjoy yourself in the company of your fellow passengers. You can check your valuables in the purser's office for which you will get a receipt. I do hope you and I will be happy all our lives together through thick and thin, dear Eva of my own. My thanks to your parents for giving you to me, and I hope I will make them happy through making you happy and contented all your life. Best Regards to all of your family, and my best love & kisses xxxxx to you dear Eva, I remain Yours own Morris x

Rev. J. Weintrobe B.A. "Rookwood"
Phone 3268

    87, Eaton Crescent,
    Swansea,
    South Wales
    18/7/38

My dear Morris,

    As you can see from the above address I am here in
Swansea. I came down on Friday & will leave here tomorrow
or Wed as I am waiting for Max & Ann to come down for a
day. Celia & Harold are also here & will go home with me.
    Dear Morris, it will not be long now before we are to-
gether again & I can hardly believe it. I have booked my passage for Aug. 5th on the "Scythia." I believe it will arrive in
New York 8 days later but find out to make sure. I had intended going on the "Samaria" which leaves Liverpool on
July 30th, but one of the girls at our shop has a brother working as steward on the Scythia & she also said it is a much better ship than the "Samaria." I told her that I had promised you
to sail at the end of the month, she replied that you would not
mind waiting for a few days longer if you knew that I would
have more comfort. I hope you are not vexed Morris, as I said
before the time will soon fly. I can hardly believe that in a
month from now I will be with you, and I am very glad &
happy about it.

I left work last Friday & received a beautiful canteen of cutlery in Electro Silver plated Nickle Silver from the girls. I had a small farewell party before I left. I have promised to go round before I leave England. I have been given a few small presents from friends, these are the first of our wedding gifts[.] I had written to Auntie Jean & told her of my getting the visa. I am also going to write again to-day to let her know when I am sailing. They have put Uncle Arthurs name on the papers as claiming me until my marr[i]age, so it may be necessary for him to [be] there to meet the boat. I wonder if we will find each other changed. The man at the shipping office said he does not think we will have to get married on the boat if Uncle Arthur is claiming me. I cannot write much as the kids are running round the place. Joe & Rosy also Celia send you their very best regards. I also send my kindest regards to your family.

With all my love to you dear until we meet again. xxxx

Your's ever
Eva

83 Chatham St.
Liverpool 7
26/7/38

My dearest Morris,

I received your very welcome letter this morning & I am answering right away. I had been expecting a letter from you all last week. As I wrote in my previous letter I am leaving Liverpool on the "Scythia" on Aug 5th. I too am very happy at the prospect of seeing you again very soon. I have been counting the weeks & soon it will be the days until we will be together again. Morris dear, I have been so very busy the last few days shopping & other things to attend to. I have to be at the Deaf Club on Friday night to receive a present from the members. I have asked for candlesticks.

I have written to Auntie Jean & am also going to write to Weintraubs and Harrisons to let them know when I will arrive. I had a few friends down for tea on Saturday & it all went off very well. I will also be having a few more down next Sat. I wish you could have been here with me to receive the good wishes. My parents thank you for your good wishes & hope we will both be very happy together. Mother is trying to take things a bit easier for my sake. I enjoyed my few days stay in Swansea[.] [O]n the way back I went to Cardiff. Max & Ann were there & we spent a very enjoyable afternoon together.

This I think will be my last letter to you before I leave England. I can hardly believe it is true.

This birthday card is postmarked August 25, 1938 from Miss E. Weintrobe c/o Harrison 813 Maple St, Brooklyn, New York

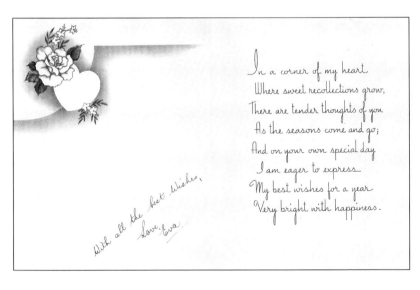

In a corner of my heart
Where sweet recollections grow,
There are tender thoughts of you
As the seasons come and go;
And on your own special day
I am eager to express
My best wishes for a year
Very bright with happiness.

With all the best wishes,
Love, Eva

Best regards to you from my parents & family. Please give my best regards to your father, sister & brother.

My best love & kisses xxxx to you dear until we meet again.

Your's own
Eva

Eva and Morris's
wedding invitation.

Mr. & Mrs. Eli Weintrobe

Mr. & Mrs. Solomon Davis

request the honor of your presence at the
marriage ceremony of their children

E v a

t o

M o r r i s

Sunday Evening, September Eleventh
nineteen hundred and thirty eight

at 7 P. M.

at **Cong. Talmud Torah Kehillas Jacob**
of **East Flatbush**
68 East 94th Street, Near Rutland Road
Brooklyn, N. Y.

Bride's Residence
c. o. Harrison
813 Maple Street
Brooklyn, N. Y.

*Eva and Morris on
their wedding day.*

EPILOGUE

The Ever After

Lennard J. Davis

The letters end with Eva, full of excitement and a bit of fear about the wedding, setting sail on the SS *Scythia*. After all the obstacles and setbacks, she must have felt certain of the course she was charting. She had overcome her doubts about Morris, her uncertainties about leaving her family, the discriminatory barriers presented by the immigration bureaucracies, and the difficulties of travel and relocation. She was set on reuniting with her fiancé and getting married to him.

She arrived in late August and was married on September 9, 1938. Morris and Eva moved into a one-bedroom apartment in the Bronx near Jerome Avenue. Gerald Julius Davis, their first son, was born on October 14, 1939. Morris continued to work as a sewing-machine operator in the garment district. Eva took in alteration work at home. Morris went on racewalking and remained part of the 92nd Street YMHA's track and field team until his death. Both Eva and Morris were active participants in the Hebrew Association of the Deaf and the Union League of the Deaf. They had many friends in the New York City area. In the 1940s they moved to Clinton Avenue in the Bronx, and on September 16, 1949, I was born.

In our household, signing was natural and deafness was

Eva's wedding portrait.

normal. My parents spoke to us in what has been called "simultaneous communication," speaking and signing at the same time. My brother and I picked up sign language in a natural way. We spoke to our parents using both sign and speech simultaneously, and funnily enough, our voices mimicked theirs, especially our mother's Liverpudlian accent. Since she had become deaf postlingually, she was the one whose verbal patterns we imitated. Morris's speech was more guttural and forced.

Much of our lives was intertwined with the Deaf club and Deaf friends. We went to the Hebrew Association of the Deaf, then on 85th Street in Manhattan, where we watched captioned films, played with other CODA children, and participated in Hanukkah parties, magic shows, and the like. Unlike many Deaf people, both my parents enjoyed having hearing friends. So we did not feel isolated within the Deaf world but moved freely between the two realms.

For us, our parents' deafness was not remarkable. Deaf culture inside and outside the home was the way life was. On the other hand, I was acutely aware of the way the hearing world then considered the Deaf world. I fought with some of my friends when they made fun of the way my parents spoke. I glared at people on the subway who stared at my parents when they were engaged in sign language conversations. I saw it as my role to defend my parents against the discrimination of the world. At the same time, I wanted very much to enter that world. So I felt both the desire to flee deafness and the guilt for wanting to do so. Now, especially in putting together this collection, I feel I can rejoin my parents and the Deaf world in a way that makes sense to me as I enter a half-century of being alive.

Before continuing, I have to let the reader know that

Gerald and Lenny.

*Morris (left) with 92nd St. YMHA teammates
in the 1960s.*

there was one letter from my father to my mother that was never sent. I learned about it when I was about ten or eleven years old. As my mother was ironing in the kitchen, with her back to us, my father decided, in his characteristically abrupt way, to tell me about the past. He said that just when Eva was about to come over on the SS *Scythia,* he had sudden misgivings. He told me how as a young man he had contracted a case of the mumps, and how when the illness was over, one testicle had atrophied. He was concerned that he was no longer fertile and decided that he had to tell Eva this in a letter before she came to marry him.[1] Dutifully, he wrote the letter and dropped it in the mailbox. Immediately, he was seized with grave doubts. He sensed the finality of what he had done, and thought that he had jeopardized his chance of marrying this woman whom he clearly adored and who had finally decided to come to the States.

After thinking for a few hours, he decided to retrieve the letter. So, he went to the post office in Brooklyn and asked to get the letter back. However, the mail had been delivered to a central post office in Manhattan. Morris rushed down to the central post office, which initially refused to consider his request. When he made a big scene demanding the letter back, gesticulating, shouting in his guttural voice, and claiming the situation was a "matter of life or death," he succeeded in retrieving the letter, which he then destroyed.

My father told me this story as I stood listening in as-

---

1. Although his explanation might have been correct, a more probable diagnosis is varicocele—an inherited condition in which a vein in the testicle becomes varicose. The heat generated from this condition can render the testicle infertile and atrophied.

Grandfather Solomon with Lenny and Gerald.

The family in 1952 at Brookstone Lodge, a bungalow colony in Hudson Valley run by Deaf proprietor David Davidowitz.

tonishment, thinking that if the letter had gone through, perhaps I would have never been born—yet another misunderstanding in the already fraught correspondence.

I don't know if my mother ever knew about this letter, even years later. I do know that there is a ten-year interval between my brother's birth and mine. My parents' had always talked about the difficulty of conceiving. I suppose I attributed that difficulty to the physiological condition my father described, although it could easily have been attributed to my parents' advanced ages, since my mother was thirty-nine and my father fifty-two when I was born.

With the absence of the missing letter, my mother came to the States with hopes, expectations, and fears. The question most readers will have is did the marriage work out? The answer is a qualified "yes." No marriage is perfect, and each one has to be defined on its own terms. From my point of view, I could have imagined a better relationship, but my parents rarely complained about each other in any serious way. For that matter, they generally did not complain about much. They were stoical people.

My mother told me a story about how shortly after my parents were married that my mother and father were getting on a bus. My father directed her gruffly to the back of the bus. When he sat down next to her, she was crying. She didn't understand how he could be so curt with her, and how she had come all the way to America and was not being treated the way she had expected. It was in this conversation that she told me about Isadore Alpers, the Leeds man mentioned in her letters, and how she might have married him. He was well-off financially, while my parents had always lived a penurious existence. I sensed in her discussion with me a feeling of regret for

"Joseph Sold," a drawing by Morris Davis.

what might have been. I asked her why she married my father, and she said, "He's a good man. He works hard, doesn't drink or beat me." That explanation seemed a long way from the sentiments expressed in the letters, but perhaps not so. Eva was always more reluctant to express her feelings about Morris than he was about her. My father was enamored of my mother until the day she died. And after her sudden death, he was heartbroken and forlorn for the rest of his life.

On the other hand, my father was not an easy man to love. He was capricious, moody, and arbitrary. His life must have been frustrating, especially for a talented man who was deaf. In those days, there was little opportunity for deaf people to have rewarding careers. My father was a talented artist, and he was encouraged to follow that career path when he was younger, but he easily ran into discriminatory roadblocks in London that made him follow the expected apprenticeship in the trades. My brother and I have wonderful pen-and-ink drawings he did from the ages of twelve through sixteen that reveal a meticulous attention to detail and a great skill in drafting. But he ended up working in Dantesque sweatshops in New York City. He put his care and craft into his sewing, and was rewarded with steady work (although always seasonal) and low pay. He was a talented actor, performing in many of the Deaf club entertainments. He wrote and directed many plays, and was a regular columnist for the national Deaf magazine, the *Silent Worker,* renamed the *Deaf American* during the post-McCarthy period. He was a gifted parliamentarian, and he was recognized by the Deaf club as such. But in the hearing world, he was just a deaf "dummy" in a menial job, on unemployment payments for half the year. His racing was the area in which he excelled in the hearing world, but as he grew older,

Morris and Eva at
Gerald's wedding, June 1972.

he had less opportunity for success. Most of the time he stayed home, read the newspaper cover-to-cover, and grew alternately depressed and agitated, neither of which he would ever admit. He was capable of great affection and humor, but more likely he was sullen, burning a slow flame of anger, easily irritable. He was stingy, and my mother's siblings all have stories to tell about how he grudged giving her money to have her hair done or buy clothing. I have no doubt he doted on her and loved her devotedly, but he would spend money on nothing, not even her.

I am not so sure about her love for him. I think she loved him the way a woman in an arranged marriage loves her husband. She began with higher expectations, but she settled into living a life parallel with his. Life was, for the most part, a colorless round of repetitions without much frivolity or sense of occasion. If asked, she would say she loved him, but it was a love without enthusiasm. I don't think she was passionate about him, although I know that they made love regularly until she died, when she was in her sixties and he in his seventies. They argued regularly, and when I was young it was my "job" to stop them from fighting. My brother would send me in so that my cute, infant presence would embarrass them into civility. Usually this tactic worked, although they always insisted that they were not fighting but "discussing." However, the emphatic signing, with its audible hand-slapping, and their involuntary verbal expostulations indicated otherwise to trained ears. I am sure that divorce was never an option for either of them, even if they had wanted it. They had Old World values.

My mother was crossing Second Avenue on September 26, 1972, on her way from the Hebrew Association of the Deaf to a luncheonette when a van came careening along and struck her. She died in the hospital two days later. My father was so distraught when he heard the news of her death that he collapsed and had to be taken to the same hospital in which she died. I never thought he would survive on his own, but he managed to live on his own into his eighties. He contracted prostate cancer, which spread to his bones and lungs. He died at age eighty-three in 1981. And so their story ended.

It started out as a romance and it ended as a tragedy. My mother's untimely death was the blow from which my father never really recovered. He had been a bachelor until he was forty and spent thirty-two years married and another eleven alone. I had hoped he would remarry, but he always said he was a "loner." He was Deaf-identified, as was my mother, but he always saw himself as having a life outside of the Deaf world as well. His racing was his link with the hearing world. Unlike many other Deaf people, he did not reject the hearing world and was not, in this regard, rejected by that world. He could have moved to Tanya Towers, a high-rise for deaf people in lower Manhattan, but he refused that option. He said he did not want to spend his whole daily life with Deaf people. He continued racing, and had his last race at eighty, three years before he died.

This story then is a small one of two people in love. It is a story, like the work of African American writer Zora Neale Hurston, that takes place almost entirely within an identity community. Like being black in Hurston's work, being Deaf in this correspondence is not highlighted since Morris and Eva are in what is called in sign language the DEAF WORLD. The letters reflect the intimate news of that world, all the more remarkably so since the correspondence occurred during turbulent historical times. The period 1936 to 1938 was one in which the storm clouds of World War II were gathering. Many people left Europe and England because they sensed the oncoming war. Yet, in these letters, like Jane Austen's novels set during the Napoleonic wars, no public events are written about. The most historical event that finds its way into the letters is the visit of the king and queen of England to Liverpool in a letter dated March 19, 1938. Yet during this period, Hitler marched into Austria, and there were pogroms in Germany beginning with Kristallnacht. Hitler occupied the Sudetenland, and Chamberlain and Hitler met. Particularly as Jews, Morris and Eva would have been noting these events, even thinking it might be better to be in the United States than in England. But the absence of these events in the letters only shows even more how the Deaf world, particularly during the prewar period, was one defined not by electronic communication but the immediate environment.

Just as novels by Jane Austen focus on the small slice of life defined by the romantic meetings of upper-middle-class and lower gentry, the letters of Eva and Morris reveal the strands in the lives of two lovers, strands made rich and complex by their very particularity. It is to that small world writ large that these letters take us, as it took them, from misunderstanding to dialogue, from courtship to marriage.